First Fault
Software
Problem Solving

A Guide for
Engineers, Managers and Users

Dan Skwire

OpenTask

Published by OpenTask, Republic of Ireland

Copyright © 2009 by Dan Skwire

Cover design: Copyright © 2009 by Nancy Skwire

Cover graphics: Copyright © 2009 by Adam Varga

Illustrations: Copyright © 2009 by Nancy Skwire

OpenTask books are available through booksellers and distributors worldwide. For further information or comments send requests to press@opentask.com.

Product and company names mentioned in this book may be trademarks of their owners.

A CIP catalogue record for this book is available from the British Library.

ISBN-13: 978-1-906717-42-1 (Paperback)

First printing, 2009

CONTENTS

"The ideal engineer is a composite ... He is not a scientist, he is not a mathematician, he is not a sociologist or a writer; but he may use the knowledge and techniques of any or all of these disciplines in solving engineering problems. "

N. W. Dougherty, *1955*

I have always enjoyed solving puzzles, of all kinds: chess, word jumbles, crosswords, word-games, murder mysteries, you name it. I was delighted to find a career early on at IBM, in solving important computer mission-critical enterprise system software and hardware problems, in-house, before customers used those systems.

After a while, the challenges, and the very fascinating technical puzzles, were in creating quality systems and in preventing problems, rather than solving whatever problems arose in the systems that were created. Over time, as described in the introduction, I got back into systems support and had to solve problems in systems that weren't pre-engineered for solving problems, not nearly as much as had been the case in my prior technical life.

This book is a synthesis of my experiences, as one who worked first building and using thoroughly engineered systems where serviceability was very strongly emphasized, and then later worked with very different systems that were evolving, and that were further back on the "serviceability" evolutionary scale. This book represents a considerable amount of experiences, time and thought devoted to original analysis regarding figuring out just what is the nature of first-fault software problem solving, and how one implements this capability into many systems, including those where these features were originally not included.

I have searched for similar books and online articles, but the guidance you are about to receive is rather unique. It is very descriptive, and meant to stimulate thought, discussion, and ultimately, action on your part. I have covered examples and thoughts from many computer platforms (operating systems and associated servers), and multiple manufacturer and vendor companies: I have intended to be vendor-neutral, and essentially "academic" in focus, and I apologize in advance for any vendor company that is not represented to the extent that they would prefer. The materials and thoughts included in this book could be used by someone creating their own operating system, or their own application program packages, but it is likely that most readers will be using industry-standard operating systems and application software.

The concepts and ideas presented are also useful for technologists who may work in non-mainstream software systems, or internal embedded software that uses systems other than Windows, UNIX, or IBM mainframes. I apologize also for the lack of numerical values to emphasize the value of the thoughts presented, but perhaps readers will be able to perform the needed controlled laboratory experiments, or analyze data they already have. I would be glad to help, and I'm very interested in their results.

DEDICATION

This book is dedicated to my family: The loving support and encouragement from my very creative wife, Nancy, and the enthusiastic cheering and encouragement from my daughter Rebekka Skwire-Cline and her husband Chris Cline.

My parents, Norma and Al Skwire, were very proud, and would be so pleased to learn that I wrote a book that was published.

ACKNOWLEDGEMENTS

"If you wish your merit to be known, acknowledge that of other people. "

Oriental Proverb

I appreciate the work my daughter Rebekka did editing this book; she has surely improved it in every way possible. My wife Nancy helped me clarify many of my ideas. In addition, she created the cover concept and did the illustrations throughout the book.

I appreciate the guidance and mentoring from many wonderful colleagues in my professional life:

During the earliest part of my professional career, at IBM, where I learned how to build, bulletproof and improve mission-critical Enterprise systems, I benefited immensely from working with: A. L. Scherr, Tony Mondello, Dave Doner, Fred Dewald, Oscar Fleckner, Regi Cardin, Sue Grissom, Merv Stump, Dave Stucki, Pam Dewey, Dick Butler, and Art Zimmerman. Later, I learned a lot about the real world supporting mission-critical customers from Robby Robison, Jim Scott, Ron Homan, Tony Ruvalo and Walt Posner.

At Florida Power, Don Higgins and Don Martin launched me into the "real world" as a customer, performing Systems Administration and Systems Programming. At Encore Computer and SUN Microsystems, I learned the joys of teaming in an innovative technology start-up endeavor: I was supported and encouraged by manager Jim Wilson, and colleagues Steve Chandler, Phil Cornelius, Julie Araki, Madeleine Slattery, Mark LeSage, Rolando Milian, Luis Morejon, Kevin Hildebrand, Ken Shaffer, Don Law, Steve Keebler, Jeff Jones, Jack Hardy, Brian Whitehouse, Mary Van Leer, and Steve Kent.

From my experiences in various formal schools, I am grateful for inspiration at all levels: Dr. Len Bass, my graduate school major professor showed me the fascinating mysteries and explanations of complex abstract computer problems. Mr. Fisher, my high school geometry teacher, left a lasting impression on the value of structure and how one solves multiple problems in forty minutes. Mr. Wallenstein, my junior high science teacher who was among the first 22 Peace Corps volunteers, enforced the rule that questions were necessary, valuable, and required of everyone. Mrs. Shapiro, my first grade teacher, encouraged me to write!

Lastly, I wish to thank my editor and publisher, Dmitry Vostokov, who originally saw the possibilities of a book, before one ever existed.

"Why do writers write? Because it isn't there."

Thomas Berger

Dan currently lives in Sarasota, Florida, with his wife, Nancy. Nearby is his daughter, Rebekka, and son-in-law Chris Cline. Dan enjoys reading and experiencing the natural beauty of the Gulf Coast shore. Dan and Nancy, a retired art teacher, both enjoy watching unusual "Indie" movies.

Dan started his career at IBM Poughkeepsie, New York in 1972, in the MVS (to become z/OS) Project Office, performing design for the MVS software recovery subsystem; the role quickly changed into Function and Systems testing of the new operating system. In 1981, Dan then performed technical sales support at IBM Tampa, Florida with a very large IBM Selected National Account. Dan left IBM in 1992 to work as a systems programmer and Unix Systems Administrator at one of his most significant customers, Progress Energy. In 1995, Dan went to work in supporting World-Wide mainframe-attached customers, both remotely and onsite for an innovative company, Encore Computer, that was building new storage array systems based upon its super micro-computers,. That storage product and organization was acquired by SUN Microsystems where Dan continued to perform product and quality support for a total of nine years. Later roles were shorter, performing problem resolution leadership in quite a variety of diverse computing environments.

Dan currently has a consultancy, "First Fault Problem Resolution Technologies LLC", where he improves clients' capabilities to solve problems on their first occurrence. He does this by special serviceability, supportability and availability studies, continuous research into best practices, studying the state-of-the-art, researching current knowledge and current and future products, and knowledge sharing by writing journal articles, speaking engagements, and this and subsequent books.

Dan enjoys thinking of being able to solve problems rapidly, on their first occurrence, as a form of technology "magic". He knows that while we can accomplish great things, we may never be able to solve 100% of problems right after they occur. However, the challenge of coming ever-closer to that 100% goal is one that Dan truly enjoys.

"He who has not first laid his foundations may be able with great ability to lay them afterwards, but they will be laid with trouble to the architect and danger to the building."

Niccolo Machiavelli (1469 - 1527), *The Prince*

CHAPTER 1 INTRODUCTION

"There is nothing more difficult to take in hand, more perilous to conduct or more uncertain in its success than to take the lead in the introduction of a new order of things."

Niccolo Machiavelli (1469 - 1527), *The Prince (1532)*

Shocked!

I was shocked! I spent many years at IBM, designing, testing, debugging, and improving computer system Recovery, Availability, and Serviceability ("RAS") features. I later set up and supported those computer systems at customer sites, and subsequently I was hired by my customer because of my ability to solve computer problems. I sure could solve problems, but they were IBM mainframe (MVS) problems. Besides MVS, the customer had Microsoft DOS, later Windows, and multiple UNIX varieties. With the Microsoft and the UNIX variants, there were hardly any message numbers to look up, and when I asked a UNIX company support center representative for help in finding the "trace table" in a storage dump, they asked me, "What trace table?"! I was starting to realize I was in a very different world.

So started the rude awakening for me, as I realized then, and for all the years following, that problem solving was just, well, *different*, in the non-mainframe world. This book represents the knowledge I have gained in my immersion in the non-mainframe world, while still retaining a "mainframe mindset". You'll see. You too will benefit by being able to apply the principles of mainframe mind-set problem-solving in your many non-mainframe environments, with computers running under operating systems like Microsoft Windows, UNIX and Linux, and others.

Mainframe mindset

What is a *mainframe mindset*, and why should you care about it? Isn't it old-world thinking, irrelevant to current systems?

No, it's not irrelevant whatsoever regarding software problem-solving, quite the opposite in fact, and you will benefit from this mainframe-mindset thinking regarding problem-solving on these different systems. Besides, recent work by Microsoft towards proactively facilitating automatic first fault problem resolution, as you will see in later chapters, has shattered the notion that the mainframe mind-set belongs exclusively to those old mainframers of last century and their old-fashioned and irrelevant technologies. Hah!

The first and most significant result of the mainframe mindset is the decided knowledge and expectation that problems *will* occur. This has far greater consequence than you may have ever considered.

But trust me; there are plenty of practical experiences which tell us that all kinds of problems will occur, as new software, with new functionality, continues to be placed into production. There are many products and systems that endeavor to help prevent but also solve problems, and we shall discuss them, but the most important value is the "mindset", the desire and goal and design principle to make sure that problems are solved rapidly when they first occur. And problems *will* occur! They *do* occur!

It is *production* problems that we care about most here: Solving the problems that occur after a system is actually put into service, whether in a cell-phone, a grid computer, a computer system operating remotely on the planet Mars (or anywhere else). Later, we will discuss what *kinds* of problems concern us, (Chapter 4 "Types of Fault, Tool Classifications, and other Design Issues").

When are problems solved?

Aren't all problems solved when they *first* occur? One wishes that were so. It is left as an important exercise to the reader to see how many attempts are needed to solve problems in his own world at his office, within his organization. Often there is insufficient problem documentation (we will discuss sufficiency later, in Chapter 4). Often one does not sufficiently examine the data one has captured, and a major challenge I have found in my many years away from IBM mainframe-exclusive work, is that people are accustomed to scheduling data collection with a specially-simulated problem event, or as I call it, a "do-over". Do-overs also will be discussed further (see Chapter 3 "Do-Overs"). Properly, professionals refer to this as "recreating" or "reproducing" the problem, but this has much meaning and impact.

Troubleshooting after a problem has occurred is time-consuming, comparatively expensive (as it requires extra hardware, software, and other resources), inefficient, and, in many cases, unsuccessful. This point was brought home in a recent article in Processor magazine, indicating that 58% of the time, "troubleshooting tools will provide IT insufficient information and will result in a problem going unresolved" (Harler, 2007). Thus, this would make quite a strong incentive to solve a problem right away, with self-identifying information. If you have to start troubleshooting after the problem occurs, the odds indicate you will not solve the problem, and along the way, you consume valuable time, extra hardware and software and other measurable resources.

When problems are expected, and efforts are made to ensure that they are solved on their first occurrence, one will have many benefits (to be discussed specifically in the upcoming chapter, Chapter 2 "Benefits").

Airplane Flight Data Recorders

The inspiration for solving very difficult problems on their first occurrence lies in the airline industry, and the creation of the airplane data recorders popularly known as "black boxes" (actually they are colored orange for greater visibility). There are many good detailed histories (L3 Aviation Recorders, 2009) but essentially, these were carried aboard by early airplane pilots for the greater good.

Data capacity and parameters captured have all been enhanced, and now flight (voice and) data recorders are mandatory in all but the smallest airplanes. They have been expanded in their capabilities, and their ability to survive the most severe crashes. The products and industries served have expanded, and they are now used in trains and ships. Also, several major automobile companies use them, and use them extensively with satellite telemetry (General Motors, 2009). The value of telemetry will be discussed further (see Chapter 5 "Software Service Tools").

Trace Tables

Very early mainframe software operating systems started using an internal "trace table", which is comparable to the black box in an airplane. Since it also captures a recent history, that is available in captured memory at the time of a computer crash, the comparisons are inevitable. IBM's z/OS (formerly MVS) operating system contained a trace table which was expanded in functionality over time, but MVS' predecessor, MVT, also had a trace table. I don't know how far back IBM's use of a trace table dates, but MVT was first available in the mid 1960's. There have been trace tables successfully used in non-mainframe systems, too, and this will also be discussed at length in later chapters (for a discussion of tracing and trace tables, see Chapter 4 "Types of Faults, Tool Classifications and other Design Issues).

Mainframe MVS serviceability design principles

In the design of the MVS operating system, circa 1972 a design requirement was that each mainline system program had a recovery program, to be invoked in case the mainline program failed (Auslander, Larkin, & Scherr,

1981). In present day's z/OS instantiation of the original MVS design, this design goal is firmly realized: all system service programs have recovery routines (Ebbers, et al., 2008). The two purposes of the recovery program are as follows:

1) Capture diagnostic data so that the original problem could be solved right after that first occurrence
2) Perform a repair function so the original error can be made transparent and the failing operation be retried, or at least, abort the failing event but enable the mainline software to be successfully re-invoked for another transaction.

The experiences testing this system's software were very valuable. If a problem could not be solved with the captured diagnostic data (purpose 1 above), then a defect was to be reported and resolved such that the failing program's recovery routine would be fixed, allowing the capture of sufficient diagnostic data, to solve the problem on the error's first occurrence. Imagine writing a defect report because a problem wasn't solved the first time it occurred. Does this happen in *your* environment? It could, and you can help. I'll elaborate more on this subject as we progress.

The above background information regarding the design principles in IBM's MVS is stated for two purposes: to explain the environment and the expectations that formed my standards and expectations, and to demonstrate what actually could be achieved practically in mainstream programming environments.

Do-overs? Recreate the problem? Not allowed! Yes, that was my expectation early in my career. At least, that was our design, our goal. Reality may have differed somewhat, and it did take a while to really approach the high standards of the design goals. Serviceability, especially first-fault software serviceability, takes repeated work and focus on the goal.

Supportability, the ability of an organization to provide support to a system, is a topic that has recently moved to the forefront. It includes serviceability, which is more oriented towards technical capabilities of providing service for specific problems. The ability to maintain a system (maintainability) is tied to supportability, which also considers the time-based long-term view of being able to support a system over its lifespan, over multiple problems, multiple improvements, and years of continuous change.

For example, in later chapters, we will talk about messages (to the computer operator or computer user) as a means of providing service information. Inconsistent and loose standards within product development regarding message formats will lead to difficulty for customers, over time, towards being able to make consistent message automation, internal documentation ("run-books"), and operator awareness. A user would like to build an infrastructure just once, around messages: he does not enjoy nor see the value in changing his environment just because a vendor has arbitrarily changed message contents. Thus, a lack of tight standards can make for supportability problems within end-user environments. Does this make sense? Supportability issues can have a very long term impact.

Capturing problem data

Is it easy to capture diagnostic data when a problem has occurred? No. The most relevant data is likely very fragile: it is likely to be re-used, over-written, modified, and the like. One is best off planning ahead; to ensure that there is plenty of data captured quickly, so that the problem *could* be solved on that first occurrence.

Planning ahead, planning for the occurrence of a failure, is a major part of the advice I'm hoping to impart. There is advice for users, including end-users and system administrators, testers, developers/software engineers, designers, and managers. One can surely improve their ability to solve a problem on its first occurrence. What needs to be improved? Software? YES! Processes used by people? YES. Can it be done in your organization? YES!

These improvements are described in two chapters. The first, regarding what users should do, is Chapter 6 entitled "What Users Can and Should Do". The second, regarding what software developers can do, is described in Chapter 7,"Creating Software With First Fault Problem Solving Capability".

Let's dig deeper into what we are talking about: *first fault software problem-solving*.

Who Solves the Problem?

First let's talk about the whole phrase: Problem solving by *whom*, you may ask? We hope that problems will be solved most rapidly and successfully by the person who experiences them. Thus, we normally think in terms of self-service. You get an error message, you look it up or otherwise research it and you perform the corrective action. Perhaps there is automation such that the message lookup is performed automatically for you: that already has been done, as we shall see.

There are some problems that are very difficult to solve – the most dramatic example is an airplane crash. The black box is the primary and sole source of continuous recorded data, and it is examined by a team of professionals, from the black box manufacturer, the airplane manufacturer, air traffic administrators (the FAA in the USA, and similar world-wide organizations). And one expects the definitive final results, not in minutes, but often, over the span of a year.

We expect faster results solving our computer problems, and we usually get them. The "we" solving problems sometimes includes computer assistance (the "cloud", database search, expert systems, et cetera).

Why is first fault software problem solving important?

WHY do we care about first-fault software problem solving? For one, there surely will be greater customer satisfaction if we solve and repair the customer's problem, or if he is empowered to solve and repair his own problem rapidly. Then there is risk minimization: Have you ever worked with a system that could not be repaired? Have you ever seen systems on the brink of disaster because their problems were unsolvable, or were very difficult to solve? Surely a technology company whose major product is a software system will be in jeopardy if that software system has unsolvable problems.

I cannot detail the extent that mission-critical unsolvable problems (some were solved) impacted the survival of the organizations that depended on those systems' functionality. In your experience, has any problem or problems threatened the success of a product, or an entire company? Make sure you do all you can to prevent this from happening from now on – continue reading!

Where? What? When? Should problems be solved on their first occurrence?

Where do we care about solving problems rapidly? Answer: Everywhere. All platforms. The world has progressed such that many people are involved with computing technologies of all kinds. Even those of us who are experts in the internal working of some computer systems, hardware or software, very often are users in another foreign system. We may be an expert on a Windows PC, but now cell-phones have very intricate operating systems and very expansive application suites. You are an important sysadmin one day, and just another user the next. This book will help you be a sophisticated multiplatform problem-solver.

What is a problem? We have used the term sufficiently. Exactly what do I mean when referring to a computer *problem*? Generally, it refers to the act of getting some unexpected or undesirable result that requires a modification. The definition is broad, as explained further, in detail, in Chapter 4 "Types of Faults, Tool Classifications and other Design Issues". We also cover the wide variety of software service tools, many of which are built-in, to solve software problems, and we interpret them for first fault software problem solving (FFSPS), in Chapter 5 "Software Service Tools".

We discuss current very important small systems software serviceability in Chapter 8, "The Special Needs of Hand-Held Computers, Cell-Phones, PDAs, and Other Small Systems". In Chapter 9 "Commercially-Available First Fault Software Service Tools", we discuss some widely accepted generally available tools that can be installed and made operational, right off the shelf.

When do we solve problems on their first occurrence? As soon as possible, of course! This subject will also be expanded. A problem solution has several critical phases, and a speed-up in problem solving will occur when you speed up any, and ideally, all of those phases. Any phases that can be done concurrently will also speed up arrival to a working solution.

First Fault Software Problem Solving – Besides immediacy, this often questions the ability to be serviced at all. Do you have system features and tools that provide serviceability information which just help in problem diagnosis and repair, or can you actually diagnose and *solve* problems on their first occurrence with those features and tools? In other words, do the products allow you to solve problems when they happen, or do the products help you along the way when you expect you will eventually solve the problem? If you don't design systems to solve problems right away, then perhaps you have no serviceability defined at all. Think about it!

We also cover the situations when problems are not solved on their first occurrence, and you need tools (see Chapter 10 "'Second Fault' Tools") to solve them on a reoccurrence that has been either trapped in production, or forced in a laboratory environment. And if the First Fault tools fail, and second-fault tools are inadequate or not appropriate, then we can discuss other means of manually, intellectually solving the problem with new ways of extracting value from the data: this is Chapter 11 "Maximizing the Value of Diagnostic Data".

Let's analyze the title of this book, "First Fault Software Problem Solving", one word at a time:

Meaning of first-fault software problem-solving

FIRST FAULT: As soon as the anomaly occurs, using information available at that time. Planning to ensure that this information is sufficient for resolution, is captured and used rapidly. Avoiding do-overs and problem re-creations as much as possible. A "first fault" is any instance where there is a situation that deviates from expected or required results.

Sometimes a fault is a problem, sometimes it can be recovered, and sometimes a fault may not be harmful occurring once but as a prediction of future faults, the earliest or "first fault" deserves attention, and should not be ignored. If there is a subsequent "problem", let's ensure we could solve it with information from the first fault.

SOFTWARE PROBLEM SOLVING: Diagnosis sufficient to avoid future failures, to repair the current failure, or both. We aim to do as much as we can with the first set of diagnostic data, understand the true causes, and actually solve the problem.

I would be delighted if every reader of this book read every chapter. However, I realize that people have to be efficient with their time, and often, a book is used as a specific reference.

In the section of the book on "The Future", we focus on leading-edge implementations and products and processes we can expect in the future.

Chapter 12 entitled "Leading Edge Software Tools" discusses several modern tools and their implications for future products.

Chapter 13 "Unanswered Questions" encourages thoughts regarding unavailable measurements of values of some of our valuable concepts, with a to-do list for the motivated reader, of very personal unanswered "first fault" questions.

Chapter 14 "Directions and Suggestions" includes some future predictions, some hopes for new products and some ideas for future process implementations.

Chapter 15, "Summary", is where we put it all together, our new knowledge of thinking, processes, tools, and our own improved standards to plan future actions to improve FFSPS in our own worlds.

What are the benefits of reading this book?

There are numerous benefits to you, the reader, when reading appropriate chapters, or this book entirely. The knowledge you will gain will make you:

1) Able to improve the service to your customers via the software you use, create or manage.
2) Able to improve the speed at which you solve computer problems
3) Able to improve products you create, regarding first fault problem solving capabilities
4) Gain the support of your management structure, colleagues and direct reports for improvements you seek. This book includes valuable talking points you will use in your discussions.
5) Able to improve your capability to anticipate needs in your organization, and the value of new products and services.
6) Able to improve the value you get from products and services and the associated vendor support organizations.
7) Able to improve quality-associated bonuses you may be awarded.
8) Able to improve your ability to control and drive the problem-solving process in your professional career.
9) Able to reduce the resources consumed in problem-solving. If you're a product developer/vendor, then you will shrink service costs. If you're an end-user of computer systems and software, this will shrink the amount of personnel and computer time and resources consumed with problem solving.
10) You will shrink the numbers of occurrences of problems by maximizing the numbers of times the problems are solved on their first occurrence.

At this point, you are now starting to see that first FFSPS is a concept which likely can benefit you and your organization, your customers and your products. In this book we will discuss some more motivation, establish basic concepts, and then get into current and future technologies for your use.

Our next chapter will examine the benefits of FFSPS in quite a variety of computing environments, including those where work and responsibility may be thought to have been delegated to someone else.

Chapter 1 Introduction

CHAPTER 2 BENEFITS

"He is great who confers the most benefits"

Ralph Waldo Emerson (1803 - 1882)

Sure, skip this chapter if you never need to ...

This chapter will go into some of the explicit benefits of FFSPS. Some readers could skip this, and go on to subsequent chapters, including the following chapter on "do-overs". Why skip this chapter?

You could skip this chapter if you already are a firm believer of first fault problem solving, and you do not need any arguments to convince your colleagues, or people who report to you (if you are a manager), or people who you report to (if you are not CIO or at the top of your company's management chain).

If you need more convincing yourself, or, if you want more arguments to convince those above or below or adjacent to you in the organization chart, please continue reading this chapter.

This chapter discusses the need for using first fault software problem solving (FFSPS), and the consequences of ignoring it. The next chapter, Chapter 3, covers a related but different topic, "Do-Overs".

Solve problems faster

It seems obvious, that to solve a problem right after it occurs, instead of sometime afterwards (after great research and potentially multiple "problem reproduction" events) is most efficient. Obvious. True.

However, can you the reader tell me how many times, on average, your organization does *not* solve a software problem on its first occurrence? Do you know what percentage of the time your HELP desk has to connect up to a user's system, either to examine their data, or to ask them to recreate the problem? What percentage of the time is a problem solved immediately after it is reported to the support organization? And what is the elapsed time from when a user experiences a problem to when that user will acknowledge that the problem is solved, and he is willing to close out the issue with your organization?

What time is consumed performing further research after a problem is reported? How much of the time is the HELP desk contacted for problem resolution? How often do users examine online help files for self-assistance in problem resolution? How often do they look up problem symptoms in your company's database? How often do they present the helpdesk with sufficient information for the HELP desk to solve the problem immediately? There are many questions here, but the answer is, for sure, even though you don't know how slowly your organization solves problems, that problems can be solved *faster* with explicitly planned products and services, which are to be described later in this book.

Conserve resources

Improvements to an organization's ability to solve problems on their first occurrence, or "earlier" than "presently occurring" will save resources. The most obvious resource saved is elapsed time until normal processing of work can be resumed. But there are other resources saved: people/personnel resources and physical resources.

By conserving "People Resources" individuals may:

- Be more efficient with their time.
- Require less involvement with HELP desk and other personnel.
- Significantly reduce labor consumed to support problem recreation resources.
- Enable the Enterprise to receive a discount, perhaps, with external support organizations (vendors). A vendor may discount the service fee for an organization that demonstrates it is well-run regarding managing problems, for being able to ensure fewer, but more well-defined problem calls. Often, a person is designated at a customer site to be the only person authorized to call the vendor support organization, and the skillful handling of problems by the coordinator is worth a vendor support discount due to various efficiencies (data collection, problem screening, symptom clarification, communications to and from the end-user, and so forth).

By conserving "Physical Resources", the positive impacts to the Enterprise can include:

- More problem solving on the first occurrence, which will allow less need for problem reproduction physical resources: hardware, software, network connections, electrical power, cooling, and office square footage for the problem reproduction equipment.
- "Greening of the Organization": a trend toward a more environmentally sustainable enterprise-wide solution, one which is conservative of physical and environmental resources.

Save the corporation

Personally, I have known, or been associated with products whose defects were difficult to solve, some to an intolerable level. I have seen companies threatened with imperiled major products when the product had what appeared to be unsolvable problems. Can you relate to those kinds of circumstances? I have seen instances where major improvements were made, some that were not made, some were made late. The timing has varied considerably. What are your experiences regarding the solving of problems at your organization?

Have you ever been involved with products whose problems were so insurmountable that they threatened the survival of the company or a major organization within the company? Surely you would be interested in reading how you could avoid such a situation!

Perform a disaster recovery

Have you ever been involved with an unsolvable problem where it appeared that the normal processing was so threatened, that discussion started regarding declaring a "production 'disaster' ", and moving work and personnel to the official disaster recovery site? It is not a desirable situation, even though it appears to be very sensible at the time. But if there are urgent disastrous problems at the current site, would it not be advantageous to perform processing safely at the disaster recovery ("DR") site (Croy & with Laux, 2008)? Sure, the DR site is perfect, unless you take your same problems with you to the DR site; if you haven't diagnosed the problem, you don't know if you are running away from your problem or bringing it with you!

Ok, the previous horror stories describe someone else's problems. They can't happen to you, your company, and your site. That is because...

Counter-arguments for nonbelievers

The following arguments are used to convince reluctant users that, yes, serviceability and FFSPS really still are a concern.

A user can say,

"I can live without extensive first fault problem-solving capabilities because..."

...Our environment is very stable

Is this the case? Sometimes it is. And you don't think you need powerful first-fault problem solving tools because you don't expect problems. Perhaps you are using a very old release of MS-DOS, for example, and it is embedded – the software releases don't change, the users don't change, the workload does not change, and the environment does not change. In this situation, yes, you could get by with minimal FFSPS. Are you *sure* you have such an idyllic environment? If so, go right ahead. If however, your environment has lots of changes, and is unpredictable, or hasn't stabilized yet, and you find yourself recreating/reproducing or "doing-over" many problems, then improvements in FFSPS are precisely what you need.

Of course, if you have a rapidly changing situation, then it could be argued that the fastest way to get to a steady state, at least as far as finding production problems with your hardware and software, is *with* FFSPS tools.

... We use clustering and failover, or other fault-tolerant solutions

One could argue that the use of "clustering" and "failover", and other fault-tolerant system architectures allow both system designers and users to not need to worry about solving problems. Problems are recovered and healed. To some degree, this is true, particularly hardware problems. With clustering, a failing component, like a CPU, has a failover "mate", which takes over the software workload from the failing CPU.

According to a recent study (Scott, 1999), redundancy can prevent only twenty percent of downtime. Also, forty percent of downtime is attributed to application failure. These results may not pertain to the environments for which you choose to employ clustering and failover technologies; if you have well-behaving software but hardware is your riskiest component then clustering would be very appropriate. These are all well worth considering – you have to know where your weak spots are and then you can appropriately buttress them.

It is true that these fault-tolerant architectures allow one to redundantly recover from a failure on a node, usually a hardware failure, and diagnosing that failed hardware FRU may be easy; however, software failures need to be solved to their root cause - they can repeat frequently if not solved and repaired and are more complex due to the nature of these systems to keep processing. Data structures that describe the failure can be over-written if they are not explicitly captured and saved. And sometimes, if a node fails over in a cluster due to a software problem, that problem could be repeated over on the recovery node.

Thus, clustering and failover make FFSPS functionality even more important due to the likelihood that failure data would be written over. If you do have a clustering solution, ask the supplier to demonstrate and point to failure data that is captured during a failover event. Has this failure data been used successfully to solve software problems?

...We use outsourcing

Congratulations! You have outsourced all or part of the responsibility for worrying about Information Technology for your organization. Your worries are over. Or are they?

Shifting the responsibility of all or part of your IT operations to an external company takes many operational worries out of your hands and into the hands of another organization. Yes, that does include solving problems. However, it still is your organization's responsibility to select the external organization, continuously evaluate them, guide them, and potentially, de-select them and in-source the work or find a better outsourcer. How effectively, how quickly and accurately your outsourcer solves problems should be a key metric in evaluating their benefit to you.

In your "due diligence" you should verify that the outsourcer is prepared for rapid problem-solving, both in data collection and diagnosis. Hopefully, the outsourcer will configure systems in anticipation of problems and use rapid automatic problem data collection methods. Regarding the servicing of your problems, you will get your best value if you understand FFSPS and you can evaluate your outsourcer in relation to this.

...We use cloud computing

Cloud computing has many similarities to outsourcing regarding how much problem-solving you have to do, understand, and/or be responsible for. But cloud computing is more complex than outsourcing. You may say, "Since our applications run "in the cloud" (or on someone else's computer, computers, or data-centers, via "software as a service" – SaaS), I don't have to worry about solving problems in my applications because someone else is hosting them."

Let's look at that statement further. Have you really offloaded problem-solving to that "vendor in the cloud"? Well, yes, but still you do care that the cloud organization is successful in solving problems.

The truth is using cloud computing is really yet another variation of outsourcing part of your IT operation: instead of hosting it in-house on your computers and having it supported by another company, or you have the work performed externally by another company completely, you have delegated part or all of your Information Technology processing to one or more remote data-centers, accessible only by the internet. Much of how we viewed outsourcing also applies to cloud computing.

Leading-edge Amazon's cloud computing organization is very transparent about public posting of the time-line of their problem solving during an outage (Amazon Web Services LLC, 2009). That is great, but you still want your "cloud" organization to solve problems as rapidly as possible. And it is not only them, but you as well: when you use the cloud, your environment has actually become more complex, not simpler. This is not to say that there aren't substantial benefits to Cloud technology, because there are: one big benefit regarding problem-solving in the Cloud is that a Cloud's organization could have more sophisticated problem-solving or problem resolution facilities than your organization could afford in-house. However, "out of sight" doesn't necessarily mean that there is nothing to be concerned about, because you do have to be concerned about Cloud problem solving and Cloud communication to you when there are Cloud problems, and you are the one with the most vested interest in keeping your own organization's systems running problem-free.

For your clients, you need to be able to articulate the extent of the outage: its' impact, its' expected duration, and any follow-on actions needed during or after the outage. If you have an alternative means of processing during a long cloud outage (you have anticipated that, haven't you?!), you need to be able to successfully move work to your alternative source and move it back when your primary cloud vendor is back operationally (do you need to test that they are really back online?).

You would want your "cloud" supplier to have the best FFSPS ability as possible. This is still your concern, and evaluating their capabilities is your concern when you select, continually renew subscriptions, and later make alternative choices. And in case part of your work is "in the cloud", and part in a local data-center under your control, you surely would want to be able to optimize first-fault problem solving in the part that is under your control. You also want to be made aware of the extent of cloud problems and their impact on your organization. You may move work to and from the cloud (Healey, 2009), as well. You must keep that option open, thus you need to be aware of problem-solving methods for that work.

Any pieces of the application still resident on your own systems are your concern, and synchronization of problem discovery and communication between the cloud and your non-cloud applications is also a concern and has increased in complexity: where and when do you start your problem-solving?

Suppose you wish to be flexible, and move some part of the work to the cloud, and leave some as "non-cloud". You need to understand the service needs of the non-cloud and the cloud work, since it could come back to be resident in your environment.

Cloud computing actually uses networking: You create a request at your site, send it via the internet to the remote servicer, which computes results, or an acknowledgment that the request was received, and then the cloud servicer website sends a response back through the internet to your site. Each of these communications, from your site to the cloud, and from the cloud, back to your site, can have a communications lag, and the transmission could actually take a route with several delays at intermediate destinations as well. This was pointed out in the recent Information Week article, by Michael Healey (Healey, 2009).

We discuss some current commercial tools available to you, to assess the current expected response time of different major routes through the internet, and network and application performance management suites available to you, in the chapter describing commercially-available tools (Chapter 9 Commercially-Available First-Fault Problem-Solving Tools).

The point is clear: although CPU processing and storage requirements can be offloaded to the cloud, your environment becomes more complex since your network is more complex, and this opens up more opportunities for reliability and performance problems, which you really need to control.

Whether *fee* or *free* (Google Gmail is free; salesforce.com is fee), the cloud you use will have strong needs for serviceability and solving problems on their first occurrence. Amazon publishes a dashboard with Cloud service status, and status history with brief outage explanations, chronologies, et cetera: Amazon also has a performance monitor to watch the performance of one's application in the Amazon cloud (Babcock, 2009).

To get to a service residing in the cloud, your request has to travel to the service's website, via the internet. And the same is true for your results – they have to travel back from the service's website to your system. The route is imprecise, and perhaps different going and coming. The performance is hard to control and to predict –you do not have a guaranteed route (Healey, 2009). There are various means to gauge the performance of the Internet - see www.internetpulse.net (Healey, 2009) with data showing current rate of measured transmissions between one Internet Service Provider and another.

Also, know that the cloud has its own performance restrictions – your work and/or data, as a user, is in the middle of the cloud, and must traverse a route to get to it (use cloud general traffic information).

If you are the provider of cloud services, you will be watched very closely for outages and performance. If you are an end-user who provides services to others, it will not be sufficient for you to tell your clients that your own service provider, in the cloud, has failed nor has problems. You will be expected to provide answers, including when application availability is expected to be restored (completion of an outage), and what the root cause of the problem was, and why such a problem will not occur again.

Thus, serviceability of this first fault within the cloud is very important, very visible, not clouded (!) or hidden at all.

This, while using a cloud, one could be tempted to say, "oh, problem resolution? That is *their* challenge (the vendor who operates the cloud environment)", but in reality, it is *your* challenge too. And life is more complex.

...The performance impact is too great for us

"The performance degradation of data-recording facilities will kill my performance and I don't have the extra cycles to consume for such a purpose." Really? What is the true performance degradation of your tool? Do you really not have any extra CPU cycles in your processor(s)?

Will the support organization ask you to "run the trace" anyhow when a problem occurs? If you have a very high-availability requirement, then the small performance overhead may be well worthwhile to prevent additional occurrences (one, two,…. many) of your original problem. Some tools have no measurable performance degradation. Do you have tools to measure performance, anyhow? Can you benchmark performance?

I have had experiences where an automatic trace that by default, always started actively when the product was activated; later a vendor decision was made to turn off the automatic start-up of the trace. This was done even though the trace was found to have only a three (3) percent overhead. Can you detect three percent degradation? Do all your servers or all your client's servers run at greater than 97% utilization? By the way, that 3% degradation was of a particular service-oriented product; the product's utilization was only a small percentage of the total CPU cycles consumed on that server, so the product's 3 % overhead was perhaps 3% of maybe 10% of the CPU.

I was initially very happy to hear that the product started with the trace active, because, as a presenter indicated, "If the customer had a problem, we would ask them to turn the trace back on, and recreate the problem anyhow, and so why not leave the trace on?"

Suffice it to say, objecting to a performance impact of a tool is not constructive – you need true performance measurements of your product, of the first fault tool, and you need a sense of the impact of multiple occurrences of a problem would be, if it were not solved on its first occurrence. You should be able to assess the total cost vs. the benefits of leaving the first fault tool inactive. Yes, there are many issues here, and some analysis of data will really help you make a good decision regarding whether or not to allow performance worries to reduce software problem-solving capabilities. The best defense to this situation is firm control over problems, and problem-solving, and strong connections to your support organizations.

That reminds me – even if you use an external vendor support organization heavily, for system hardware, software, or application support, an appreciation of FFSPS and related processes will enable you to get best support from your support organization. You will be able to help them best solve your problems. Thus, you can benefit significantly from proper attention to your own, or your vendor/supplier's first-fault software problem solving capabilities.

Use these arguments to convince peers, direct reports and managers to whom you report, that analysis and attention to serviceability will benefit your organization; the consequences of avoiding this area could be severe and threaten your organization in many ways.

We now move to the next chapter for a side-issue, the issue of performing problem re-creation (or as I have called it, "do-overs"), as an alternative to focusing on first-fault software problem solving. We need to analyze do-overs, find out why we rely on them, and then move on, to proper use of existing in-house first fault features and tools, building our own or acquiring commercial tools, or planning for future tools yet to be made available.

Chapter 2 Benefits

CHAPTER 3 DO-OVERS

"We're Gonna Need a Bigger Boat"

-originally used by well
known actor Roy Scheider
in the 1975 blockbuster
Jaws.

"Do-overs?!"

Often, in the course of working on a problem, a support organization or support person will ask the person reporting the problem to "re-create it", or "reproduce it", and write down and capture the steps to recreate the problem and send it off to the support person. At times, the support organization, with a basic description of the problem, will endeavor to reproduce the problem in its own separate special laboratory computer system environment.

The laboratory computer system environment is often called a "test" environment, but it should represent the "production" environment as closely as possible: often there are differences, in load, in volume and nature of data, in software revision and version levels, and so on. As "production" changes rapidly, it is very hard to maintain an accurate "test" environment.

At times, the support organization and the end-user will both be trying to re-create the problem. And then, sometimes, the problem re-creates itself in the production environment because the problem has not been solved with sufficient time to install a problem preventive measure in place before the problem reappeared in production. I call this problem reappearance requirement a "do-over", and I will describe in detail what this really means, and now, why this process is used.

The request is so automatic these days, I am sure many people have no understanding of any other way of life to solve a problem. If you feel that way, or work with people who feel that way, then this chapter is very important to you. It is not necessary to re-create *all* problems in order to solve them!

Systems can be designed, and supported with features, such that a problem can be easily understood and resolved upon its first occurrence: Surely, if a problem does turn out to be a duplicate of a known problem, then there should be sufficient means to capture problem symptoms of the current problem instance and match them with symptoms and solutions to the previous prior instance of the problem.

Microsoft appears to have done plenty of this in the last ten years, and as a result they came a long way in solving mission-critical problems.

From my long-term perspective, working with early mainframe software systems, and then later with PCs and UNIX systems, the culture of "reproduce the problem/re-create the problem" originated with the early PC and UNIX systems. Mainframe systems were designed from the start to be used by major corporations, and as business machines, businesses relied on their successful operation and rapid repair. This impacted the design: systems utilized error messages, error-checking, preventive maintenance, et cetera, all the best practices to keep systems operating most effectively.

DEC/VAX, Wang, PC and UNIX systems were originally intended as single-user, personal systems, constructed rapidly, with an emphasis on creative application development. There was no initial plan for them to be used in mission-critical environments, as they are today. Thus, error-checking, error messages, fault tolerance, and related problem-solving tools, were added, long after the systems were initially deployed.

The cultural aspect remains today, with those DEC/VAX, Wang, PC and UNIX systems used for rapid deployment of creative applications, with an emphasis on personal tools for software application development, and many tools designed for second-fault (re-created problem) analysis and debugging.

Potentially the greatest problem, and the biggest stumbling block to greatly creating and using first fault problem solving tools in these (formerly) personal-systems-only environments is the past behavioral habit for problem reproduction. I am a techie, I am not a sociologist, but I can make this observation about my colleagues' behavior. This book and the logical arguments within are an attempt to change the behavior. Perhaps you will help, too!

Thus, it is a cultural, behavioral, almost reflex action that many people working with Windows, PCs and UNIX x86 systems tend to think right away in terms of "reproducing/ recreating" the problem. You must think about your own personal pre-disposition. How much analysis do you do before you turn to reproducing the problem?

Of course, it can be very valuable if you successfully can reproduce the problem. You can test out many alternatives for a fix or workaround, and choose the best one. Actually, the detailed steps involved in problem reproduction have been described very well (Zeller, 2006). If you have to reproduce the problem, *then*, I hope that you will use this knowledge to help prevent the next person with this very same problem from having to go through all the same steps you took. You will, won't you?!

If you do have to re-create the new problem to solve and fix it, then you can and should create a knowledge-base article, or some kind of note, in the problem database, that will allow someone searching with matching symptoms to find your problem description with the resolution/solution you have created with a means of verifying a match. Besides the knowledge article, which should be viewed as only a temporary step, you should forward the problem symptom and resolution and any tools or scripts you developed on to your development organization so the concept is put into the "queue" of future product or tool enhancements, to replace the knowledge-base article when successfully implemented.

But if the problem is not a brand new, unique problem, and the current problem could be matched with a current problem (and its solution) then do you really need to re-create it? No, you don't. And many problems are not readily reproducible, besides.

But re-creating the problem should not be done automatically, as if rote, by problem solvers. Much, much more effort should be devoted to creating methods to recognize, match, understand and resolve problems right after they first occur.

Thus, it is with some teasing, some criticism, some convincing, some imploring, that I refer to problem reproduction as a "do-over", the title of this chapter.

It is a matter of intent, and focus, that prior mainframe systems had significant serviceability function for first fault software problem solving (FFSPS). It doesn't mean that problem reproduction was never required, because it surely was, as was physically modifying the software itself ("instrumenting the 'kernel' ", also known as the mainframe MVS "nucleus"). But the intent and design focus was in place to greatly minimize the need for problem recreation. And there was a strong loop, where unsolved problems and problems that needed reproduction initiated major thoughts toward creating serviceability improvements to solve such problems immediately.

Question: Are there appropriate times to perform problem reproduction? When is it appropriate to use problem reproduction?

Answers:

1) When you are solving a hardware problem, and the solution seems likely to be in the replacement of one failing component with a

working component. One troubleshooting technique is swapping parts and seeing if the problem "heals" or disappears. If the problem has disappeared, then the part swapped out is the failing part, and the part you used for the trial is the correct replacement part. Of course, this method can be crude, and if many parts are involved as potential root-causes, then this could take a while. Additionally, this will fail if there are *multiple* parts that have failed at the same time or if one part's failure triggers a later failure in another part. But generally, this technique is used quite successfully by hardware repair personnel. This is discussed further in Chapter 11: "Maximizing the Value of Diagnostic Data".

2) If you have no serviceability tools for first-fault problem-solving. Then you must perform two activities: re-create the problem *and* create new data collection and analysis tools.

The problems with performing problem-recreation are...

1) It can be very difficult to re-create the problem that occurred. This is the first step in your process. It is very difficult to know all the conditions sufficient to re-create a problem. It requires skill, some guessing ('guestimating") and often, some persistence in repeatedly trying different combinations of conditions to cause a problem to re-occur.

2) It takes time. Even if you are very successful in rapidly re-creating the problem, it still consumes time at your site (you the end-user), or at the support organization's site. Given enough time, perhaps all problems could be replicated, but often one does not have a near-infinite amount of time, and an explanation and resolution are needed quickly.

3) It is inefficient. The first step is re-creating the problem. A second step is designing the special serviceability tool or data gathering options on existing tools to capture the data sufficient to solve the problem. The process is iterative (and time-consuming). If you haven't debugged the problem the first time you recreated it, you must re-create it again, with a different, or an enhanced/improved tool. Perhaps the new tool or script needs to be debugged too, before it can successfully capture the data from the reproduced problem.

4) In production, trying to capture diagnostic data regarding the problem's second occurrence could be dangerous. Technical personnel have known to modify their product ("instrument the kernel") to

capture data that the product never gathered before. This is likely new code that never ran in production before, and it might crash the computer or just some production process; the first time around the modifications might just not successfully capture the desired data. Thus, problem reproduction can sometimes lead to many additional failures and the need for further software development work and more problem reproduction efforts.

5) Often the informal product modifications used to capture data for a particular problem are discarded or saved by an individual privately. They are not easily re-used, and for sure, are not incorporated into the product to prevent re-creation of the debugging code. There is a great consumption of person-hours that could have actually been redirected and considered an investment in a product service improvement.

6) Recreating the problem implies stopping normal processing short, perhaps, in a test lab, or in production. When normal processing is stopped, you have to be careful, because you might have prevented recovery or follow-on processes from occurring in the problem reproduction, so just debugging from the lab environment could inhibit you from examining how the problem behaves with all its impact in production. You need to be careful when you stop your lab reproduction process.

7) Sometimes, reproducing the problem is not practical. When a Mars landing robot and its computer failed, how and where could one reproduce the problem (Associated Press (AP), 2009)? What test-lab? Would any conditions have to be simulated when the Mars rover problem is re-created?

8) Re-creating the problem is error-prone. You might re-create symptoms of the problem, but actually have created a different problem with common symptoms. Your subsequent work would not be valid. You could cause damage to a product or test environment, or even a production environment, trying to re-create the problem and setting up resources to collect diagnostic data. You may have created a fix that does not work because you recreated a problem with a symptom matching the original problem, but with a different root cause.

I often think of the games I played as a child, in a sandlot, unsupervised. We had no referee, so whether a ball was "in-bounds", or "out-of-bounds", was a judgment call. If the two competing teams couldn't reach an agreement on the outcome of a "play", then we would perform a "do-over", except, it was never quite the same event. The original event could never truly be "done over". "Do-overs" were unsatisfying to me, even then.

It is this difficulty that I ascribe, I am sorry to say, to "problem re-creation". It is problematic, inefficient, and error-prone, and when possible (keep reading!), should be avoided for more proactive and logical methods. I so strongly encourage a focus on maximizing usage of first-fault tools, as well as development of improvements in first-fault software problem solving solutions.

A "Do-Over" is surely not the same, whether it is re-doing the presidential oath of office on January 21, 2009 (instead of the official date on January 20th), or resolving a problem on a computer system. Even if a perfect problem reproduction occurs rapidly, this "do-over" is still time-delayed, and it may not prevent a production reoccurrence in sufficient time.

System "YUK"

This is a good time to introduce my favorite poster-child for the world's worst system regarding software serviceability. It is a "straw man" (Korach & Mordock, 2008) that I call System "YUK". This is not an acronym. It is just named to signify my distaste for this very hard to service, very poor quality system. I'm sure that you will find YUK distasteful, too.

System YUK is very complex. It makes many decisions, and analyzes much data. However, the only means it has of conveying an error it has detected is the single message to the operator console, "**SYSTEM YUK HAS DETECTED AN ERROR**". Unfortunately, due to the lack of maturity of YUK, it conveys this error message fairly often. System YUK has no first-fault tools, so to diagnose problems in YUK, you must re-create the environment in your YUK test-bed, and add instrumentation (write statements, traces, etc) and various tools to get a decent explanation of problems with YUK, or setup some second-fault tool to capture more and better data on the production System YUK.

Imagine your favorite personal computer, Apple or Microsoft or Linux, reduced to the level of YUK: All of the messages would just say ("ERROR!"): no more, no less. Would it be easy for you to work with your favorite system with ALL details of an error message reduced down to the single "ERROR!" message? I don't think you'd enjoy working with that.

Once the problem is diagnosed, you remove the serviceability code and products, and System YUK remains just as you originally found it. System YUK represents the highest degree of problem-reproduction conceivable. All System YUK problems need to be recreated in order to be solved. There are no problems that can be identified as an already-seen problem (no symptom-matching).And every problem starts all over, with no archived collection of problem-solving tools.

I am not really claiming that YUK is the secret name for any commercial product, because it isn't! Surely you'll agree with me that YUK is the world's worst system. Hopefully, nothing you work with strongly resembles YUK. However, as our poster-child, we aim to prevent any of your systems from resembling YUK, and in essence, this book will tell you how you can use products and processes to prevent you from ending up with YUK.

Think about this: We are talking about problem reproduction. If you have to rely on problem reproduction almost exclusively, does your product have any serviceability of its own? Is it possible you could wind up in one of those "death-spirals" of problems compounding, with resolution continually delayed such that you are in a risky situation with many unsolved problems and an Enterprise at great risk to being consumed by such problems? I do not wish to panic you, but think, think about your organization's exposure to rampant unsolved complex destructive problems.

System TROP

System TROP is another "straw man", but its problem is that it is very descriptive in its serviceability information. As a matter of fact, system TROP is at the other extreme of System YUK: System TROP conveys so much status, and collects so much information, that's almost all it does. It gives status messages for every decision made in the operating system, and every I/O interrupt, every dispatch of a unit of work, and so on. And it traces every instruction and every decision that is made. More commercial systems have some affinity with system YUK than with system TROP, but system TROP is included for completeness. Yes, "trop" is the French word for "too much".

From personal experience, it is possible to use very highly skilled, trained and educated personnel to perform the difficult job of problem recreation: these personnel are highly skilled and educated because many diverse intellectual skills are needed for successful problem recreation, more so than less-skilled support persons interpreting well-architected error messages, especially if users could do it! One could think that there would be higher costs associated with having support people frequently recreate problems vs. those would need to do that minimally. With all their skills and expertise, the funny thing is that the presence of these highly-skilled professionals actually allows the development and enhancement of first-fault software service tools to be neglected, when problem reproduction is the standard problem solving method!

So, design and development personnel costs for the first fault software tools are not consumed if you don't have true first-fault problem-solving facilities, but costs accumulate with extra personnel efforts on the service side. You have to pay for the cost of processing some minimal amount of problem-solving logic, somewhere, somehow! Plus, one could argue, that customers would need substantial vendor service support, because the products are not as easily serviced by customer technical personnel: there are fewer opportunities for easy "self-service". Products whose vendors skimp on first-fault software serviceability development costs spend more on service, and so do their customers!

It is with a sense of the humor of the situation that I think of "The Journal of Irreproducible Results" (Sperling, 2009). I discovered this magazine while a graduate student, and it was enjoyed even more by my colleagues who were in the biological sciences, particularly Oceanography studies. From its title, and many articles, you can see that the work of biological scientists (and the graduate students, the scientists-to-be) was frustrating since it was very difficult to have controlled repeatable scientific experiments with complex living organisms as your subjects. Thus, the reference to "irreproducible results"! Scientists pride themselves on being able to perform experiments and demonstrations whose results could be repeated world-wide, but "irreproducible results" are not sought after!

As a graduate student, I spent my time with computer software and hardware and mathematical logic, where repeated inputs always provided the same output and it was comparatively easy to recreate those inputs and get that same output. As a "computer guy", I did not have "irreproducible results", but I empathisized with my colleagues who did.

Still, problem reproduction in software is not so easy. You don't start with *all* the inputs that got you that output (the problem). You start with an output, an outcome, and you have to deduce, infer, and induce, etc, all the necessary and sufficient inputs to create that problem. This is surely a lot of work if you have insufficient data to debug the problem on its first occurrence.

Similarly, besides the difficulty and complexity of software problem reproduction, one suffers the possibility of being ridiculed for their "science project", going off on an expedition to re-create a problem. What happens in a student science project? In industry, I have a common language referring to a "science project" as a technology without maturity, without a group of practical production users, "in sight". For schoolchildren, a "science project" is an adventure, where the road travelled about the process and personal self-discovery is far more important than the result. In industry, it's the *results* that are important. In solving computer software problems, the result is very important, as well as accuracy. Don't let your software problem-solving get compared to a science project!

Do-overs have a cost, and a major impact. They should be de-emphasized as an exclusive means of solving so many problems. Focus on getting a rapid diagnosis, not a series of open-ended tests. Use technology to create and use first-fault problem solving tools.

Let us move on to discuss our problems and the technologies we can use to solve those problems rapidly.

"I've come up with a set of rules that describe our reactions to technologies:

1. Anything that is in the world when you're born is normal and ordinary and is just a natural part of the way the world works.

2. Anything that's invented between when you're fifteen and thirty-five is new and exciting and revolutionary and you can probably get a career in it.

3. Anything invented after you're thirty-five is against the natural order of things."

Douglas Adams (1952 - 2001),
The Salmon of Doubt, p. 95

CHAPTER 4 TYPES OF FAULTS, TOOL CLASSIFICATIONS AND OTHER DESIGN ISSUES

"The greatest of faults, I should say, is to be conscious of none."

Thomas Carlyle (1795 - 1881)

In this chapter, we will describe the kinds of faults that are experienced in general purpose computer systems, and we describe the kinds of information needed to solve the problem. We also give some classifications of the kinds of tools used to gather the information to solve such problems.

Service Points

I like to establish the concept of a "service point", which is a place in a computer program where a particular important condition is detected. For example, if a programmer tests a status indicator, a "return code" from invoking another program, and finds an abnormal condition (by convention, that is a "non-zero" return code), then the program detecting the non-zero return code could take an action. Often this is the place where, for a very critical program invocation, where a message is written, usually to the user or operator of the computer system. The service point could mark a problem area (non-zero return code for example), or a major positive milestone (start or completion of a unit of work). Service points are valuable.

Although our friend, system "YUK", has many service points, it sends out the same message from all of them. It is possible that at a critical service point, where important information is detected, that a program does not write a message to the user. This is a lost opportunity, and one that makes servicing the associated program more difficult. If a problem occurs, one might consider rerunning the program (yes, a "do-over"), with WRITE statements inserted at multiple service points, to find out if anyone of them yield a non-zero return code.

One would expect that a more serviceable system would have a way of recording critical non-zero return codes for later problem-solving. This is not really a minor point. Highly serviceable systems have ways of communicating the results at service points – some systems (like many Unix variants) write messages to the user, but also each component part of the Unix system has its own associated message log, which is a separate file on disk.

Service points are very usable places to establish and collect serviceability data, even if the current software system does not issue a message or generate a failure code there. You might find yourself setting up to "trap" or "catch" a software system at particular service points when and if you have to recreate the problem.

Types of faults

Synchronous errors

Faults that are revealed at service points are also known as "synchronous errors". A program has detected an error condition and synchronously, immediately conveys that to the user (human or automated/electronic). These synchronous errors mark where processing has essentially stopped to report the error. The opposite kind of error, an "asynchronous error", will be more difficult to solve since you don't know when the real problem started, just when or where the symptoms got bad enough to be detected.

Most systems with an operator display, a console, use messages to the operator, and we discuss the use of messages in the next chapter, in more detail. There are ways to get maximum advantage from messages.

Abort Codes and ABEND codes

Other systems convey a synchronous error via generating a system error code (Microsoft Windows), abort (UNIX term), or an ABEND (Abnormal End – an IBM z/OS term). Often these errors have associated numbers (abort number, termination code, ABEND code). The abort starts termination of the program, the unit of work in the associated operating system environment. This is often a more severe error than would be associated with a message alone.

For an abort, the program can no longer continue processing. It is ended, and usually, a storage dump is captured. Microsoft operating systems have this concept, too, and they do capture dumps. The contents of these storage dumps are very interesting, and they are solved by technicians with deep knowledge, since the dumps are often in a binary number format – ones and zeroes – 1's and 0's (or a reformatting like an octal or hexadecimal format). Storage dumps are important, but are definitely not user-friendly.

Stop Codes and Wait state codes

When a system has encountered an error which cannot be bypassed, either without jeopardizing data integrity, or because mandatory structures may be compromised, it can enter a stopped state. An informative message with a numeric code can be displayed to the system user console/display. This technique is used by Microsoft Windows (stop codes), and by IBM mainframe z/OS (wait-state codes).

Other service points indicate that the error is so severe, such that data integrity could be compromised, and data could be corrupted, if processing were to continue. This causes a stopped state in the system. In the IBM z/OS world, this is indicated by a "coded wait state". Other systems have similar error messages.

Some systems communicate the need for critical action and then allow further processing (restartable wait-states). Surely, your favorite system will have its own unique methods of using codes to depict status.

User storage dumps

Depending on the kind of problem, and the detecting component, one usually can obtain a user storage dump. Storage dumps contain a complete picture of the total state of the associated user (or system). As a first fault tool, a storage dump has all the data: it may not be easy to read or interpret, but once captured, it is very valuable compared to other kinds of diagnostic data. As with all other storage dumps, the storage dump is a picture at some point in time: how and when different parts of the storage got altered is not apparent. The answer to "how did we get *here*" (to this particular state of storage) is answered with a "trace".

Also, since capturing the storage dump is a dynamic process that occurs over a relatively short period of time, it is possible that some data areas in the storage dump can be over-written before they are sent to the output device. It takes a lot of work to get a good picture of the storage state in a dynamic system. Think of it as using a slow-speed shutter to take a photograph. If the object being photographed is moving rapidly, you will get a blurred image – the same problem is possible with a storage dump in a very active system; you will get the equivalent of a "blurred image", in the more active, frequently, changing areas in the storage dump.

But a storage dump is surely a very important picture.

System Area Storage Dumps

Microsoft Windows, UNIX variants, and IBM mainframes all have a means of obtaining a very complete system dump. The system dump is usually much larger than a user dump, since the system dumps contain large, common system data areas, and may contain all user areas too, while the user dumps contain a single user's memory area. Some UNIX variants, and also IBM z/OS allow for concurrent non-destructive capture of a system dump – z/OS provides synchronous data capture from a "recovery routine", upon detection, at a service point, of a critical problem. z/OS also captures volatile data during this process.

With UNIX and Windows, one must ensure that a system is pre-configured to capture that dump at the time of an error. Else, a dump is not captured, and a first step in problem reproduction is to configure the system to capture that dump. Get the dump, either now, or later. If a dump is needed by the support organization, you will have to configure to capture it, and then hope the problem re-occurs, or force it yourself, if the support organization can't re-create it. Since processor storage is comparatively large in current implementations, storage dumps can be requested in full, or variously abbreviated or selected sizes in many platforms.

Crash dumps and standalone dumps

UNIX and Windows systems have a means to capture the system state by uploading the memory contents to a peripheral storage dump file usually on disk – sometimes located on a remote server, but also magnetic tapes have been used. These storage dumps can be later analyzed by a specialized analysis program, formatting key system and/or user data structures, providing various amounts of insight. Some dump formatters just lay out the data structures with the field names of the data areas, but others provide deep intelligence, comparing the values in the data structures with norms, and they can report on the general health of the underlying programming component, with maxima and minima of the observed values.

Often in Windows and UNIX, the storage dump is destructive; that is, the dump is taken after the associated live operating system is terminated, but SUN's Solaris allows for an additional kind of dynamic system storage dump while the user is still operating – it is non-destructive. IBM mainframe z/OS has also had a very extensive dynamic storage dump facility, and it has captured much of the volatile storage data of the failed program.

z/OS has a feature to manually capture system storage destructively, by loading what is called a "standalone dump" into a reserved place in memory, and it can capture all user virtual storage as well as real storage, to an auxiliary device (disk or tape).

Hypervisor storage dumps

When running a hypervisor, one has control over the "guest" operating system, and one can often freeze such a system, capture a storage dump, and then continue operation. These capabilities can be used in x86 platform hypervisors – VMware, XEN, Microsoft, and SUN. If one is using a mainframe virtual machine hypervisor, "z/VM", one could capture all of storage via its storage capture tool. The use of hypervisors can be very powerful in first- and second-fault problem resolution.

I/O Error

Often, devices attached to a server experience errors when the server communicates with it. These are often conveyed to the server and then server creates an error message, an ABEND code, a wait state, etc, to convey this synchronously-detected error. I/O devices can also yield asynchronous errors, to be discussed a bit later.

Hardware error

Much hardware has great internal error-checking, including parity checking, and interface checking, etc. Errors can be automatically repaired (a single or double-bit error repaired with the use of an error-correcting code and redundant bits in the data), for example. Many systems record these repair and recover events and surely should report uncorrected errors. Sometimes the report of an error indicates that part of a component is unavailable (such as half of a cache memory that is inoperative) – this will be useful because it could be the root cause of a performance slow-down.

Asynchronous errors

Sometimes, an error is detected, but it is not directly related to the work that the server is processing at that moment in the instruction stream. In other words, the currently running program is really a victim of a fault detected and reported while it is running. This can come from an error experienced by an I/O device, or an attached processor (multiprocessing). The receipt of this error information and its interpretation is still done in a system service point.

Errors *not* immediately detected at service points

As you might expect, these are your more difficult kinds of errors to solve. In terms of time and instruction execution, these kinds of errors occur a long time (in computer time) before their effects are noticed. These may require special tools to solve, and perhaps deeper analysis. We will talk more about special tools in the later chapter.

These problems are:

Hang

A computer gets into a "hang" condition when all work stops, and it appears that the system is waiting for some event to occur. Perhaps it is a response to a critical error message that has not been acted upon. Sometimes the system is waiting for the replenishment of a critical resource that has been depleted.

In any event, the state of the system is that no work is being processed, there is no indication of an obvious error that has occurred, and the CPU utilization can be very low. The actual cause of the error may have occurred over time, as could be the case with buffers that got depleted, or it may have occurred rapidly, such as with a critical I/O hanging, or it could have been a major event that happened a long time ago but was undetected.

Solving a "hang" problem would often involve monitoring of the use of important resources, and researching if some resource shows continuously-increasing consumption. Often, the problem could be solved by an external monitor of critical asynchronous events that are yet to be resolved.

Incorrect output

By "incorrect output" here, we refer to the output of computer programs that is deemed incorrect by a human analyst. The computer program is unaware of any error condition, and it completed normally doing what it was programmed to do. These problems are often difficult to solve, since one needs to know the behavior of the program, where the particular faulty outputs' component inputs were processed to create the (faulty) output.

This kind of problem could be resolved by re-coding the failing program and placing various "WRITE" statements in it. Pre-planning for such an eventuality as incorrect output would allow intermediate results to be recorded in a file somewhere to yield clues as to where processing may have erred. This, we argue to generate more output to provide for easier serviceability. Note that we are creating data to be outputted at places in addition to service points where low-level anomalies could be detected. We want more data collection in normal processing.

Some programs will allow for "DEBUG LEVELS", or "verbosity" (this term is often used in UNIX systems), indicating a variable amount of output for diagnostic purposes. Note that one could run with some initial levels of output to be generated (a non-zero DEBUG LEVEL, or non-zero "verbosity level") and you would have a first fault tool. But if you choose to run without collecting diagnostic data at all, and then later turn on various DEBUG LEVELs or verbosity, then you are using the facilities as a second-fault tool.

Performance Problem

A performance problem shows itself when a system is running its normal workload more slowly, or at maximum utilization, is running less work. There is usually no obvious symptom (for example, loss of part of the hardware complex – running with fewer CPUs than normal). Usually the primary hardware components of a computer system are CPU, processor storage, I/O devices including network devices. And they are all functioning properly – everything is slower, but what is consuming the extra resource(s)? And what extra resource(s) are being consumed?

A normal running system uses balanced portions of each hardware unit. An abnormally running system has overconsumption of one or more resources, resulting in what is often referred to as a "bottleneck". Finding the root cause of the bottleneck can be difficult.

Often a trace of resource utilization is made and recorded, with varying levels of verbosity. But if nothing has changed (nothing is known to have been changed), then the problem becomes very difficult, and it surely is difficult if there has been inadequate resource utilization monitoring. Often, visual graphs of the consumption of resources over time provide the clue: one sees a spike in the curve, or one may see a steady increase in utilization of a resource.

User error

We refer to a "user error" as really a miscommunication between the supplier of the software (or hardware) product – the vendor, manufacturer, creator, etc. – and the end-user. These kinds of problems can be resolved with better communication to the end-user: clearer documentation via book, web-site, messages, and others. But conveying the extent of the user error to the organization that will service and fix it may require great amounts of information. The vendor needs to provide a means for the end-user to collect information to send to the vendor organization. The next chapter will describe some of the most critical kinds of information, and how vendors can have their users collect and send this information to them.

Aging problem

An aging problem can often be confused with the next type of problem to be described, the "memory leak". But in essence, an "aging" problem occurs when over time, a normally functioning system stops running because a critical resource gets consumed completely. This can be as minor as just a mere counter. I remember an early aging problem that surfaced when an early operating system started to stay up for a long time, without crashing. The long time was 21 days, at which point a counter overflowed. The system operates normally, and then, all of a sudden, it will crash because a certain duration of time or numbers of events, has transpired: this describes an aging problem.

To solve the crash, one needs a complete dump of the system or application that has crashed. A trace of critical resource usage may be helpful, but since one does not know in advance what resources to monitor, it is generally difficult to pre-plan for an aging problem, other than to get a complete storage dump at the time it occurs. Regular non-destructive online storage dumps taken during normal operation could be compared with the final crash dump. In addition, monitoring and recording the consumption of various resources could be helpful.

Memory leak

A "memory leak" is a problem where memory gets over-consumed (Van der Linden, 1994, pp. 184-186). It could be as simple as a key program obtaining 40 bytes of data, and then freeing 36 bytes of data. What results is four bytes of data that is still allocated, and if not automatically freed when the program ends, you can be left with many useless four-byte blocks of data (plus several bytes of data for management information) that can be unusable since the bytes may not be contiguous. Thus, storage gets fragmented – all the freed storage is available, but the pieces are so small to be unusable by requestors who need a block larger than four bytes. The memory is just "in limbo", not really practically usable by other programs, and secretly owned by a program that doesn't really remember that it owns the storage: that program has thought that it has freed the memory it owned.

This surely is a bug, but it is not an uncommon bug, and it can be difficult to solve, since in a complex multi-user system, much storage is rapidly gotten and freed. It could be a big performance degradation to monitor and track each unit of storage obtained, but there are tools to make the process simpler. Memory leaks are common to many operating systems, even though the tools and techniques may vary.

The end-result of a memory leak, depending on whether it involves rapidly-obtained storage or not, may be a gradual degradation of performance, as the queues of allocated storage grow larger, and every request for storage requires a longer and longer search through those queues for usable storage.

Storage overlay

A storage overlay occurs when a program stores into a data area that is actually allocated to another program or function, the victim. The victim winds up with a value, or values, of data that it cannot interpret, and may not have expected, leading to very erratic symptoms. There are system designs to prevent this from occurring, with users isolated and their storage protected from one another, but operating systems need access to all user data areas, even just separate parts of them, and operating system bugs can have great impact for storage overlays.

Defensive programming (examining data for correctness and reporting via a service point can reduce the possibility of storage overlays, but storage overlays can and do happen in all systems).

Speed of problem-solving

If we are going to discuss tools and methods for problem-solving, we must consider the total speed to solve a problem. If we had infinite time, and infinite money, computer resources, personnel and infinite client patience, and minimal availability requirements, then the fault solving capability of System YUK would be just fine.

However, we live in the real world, and we know that "time is money". Yes it is, and excessive and preventable downtime represents a loss of real money that can threaten you and your organization's survival in a competitive economy. Of interest is a recent study (Information Technology Intelligence Corporation, 2009) that showed that in a blind survey an overwhelming 81% of Information Technology managers and executives are unable to quantify the cost of downtime. As ITIC stated in their title, "Ignorance is not bliss"!

The cost of the lack of availability of IT applications is really complex. There are various costs that are accumulated when systems are "down". Obvious is the cost of people who are being compensated, but are unable or delayed in performing their work because the computer system they depend upon is "down". Then there is liability from external customers who may or already have contractual penalties that have to be paid if systems are unavailable. Finally, there is lost business, such as the classical example of an online airline reservations system that generates thousands of dollars an hour, but whose customers could easily switch to another airline if there is a service outage. These concepts were explored in the 1980's in various works by IBM (IBM Corporation).

Many people are familiar with what is now a common description of a **computer outage**. To review, in a computer outage (or any other system's outage, really), there are generally a few key phases. They are:

1) Problem occurs
2) Problem affects systems
3) Problem is detected (by human or automated operator)
4) Action plan is created to solve the problem
5) Problem solving starts
6) Problem solving ends
7) Solution is tested in an alternative system, if available
8) Solution is placed into production failing system
9) Failing system is restarted
10) Work that was in progress is recovered
11) All work is back to normal.

This is a somewhat generalized informal description. The duration of the outage is the difference between the timestamps of event (2) and (11). It really can be quite long. In an Information Technology Infrastructure Library (ITIL) / "Systems Management" technique known as "outage analysis" (Marquis, 2009), one tries to minimize this time (we also try to prevent the problem, but assuming a problem can and does occur, we try to minimize the duration of the outage). This is generally a management study, where you go back and analyze, as best as you can, critical outages and try to see how you can minimize the durations of each step in the outage so that future outage occurrences will proceed faster than the actual outages that have previously occurred.

For our purposes, I want to focus on steps 1) through 6) – from when a problem occurs, to when the problem has been solved. There are many tools that can help each step:

1) The problem occurs – With ongoing data collection tools and system features, you may already have collected information that could lead you to solve the root cause of the problem. That's if and only if you have planned for proper first fault problem solving. We will discuss these system features and tools in more detail.

2) The problem affects systems – With monitoring tools that check on the state of key system components, you can have a short-hand description of the state of key components, and a time-stamp of when the system, and particular component(s) are adversely affected. Plus you can have a good picture of the state of those systems.

3) Problem is detected (by human or automated operator

   Surely you want a means to communicate to a human operator or support person. Besides an operator display screen (an "operator console"), perhaps, email notifications to the operator, cell-phone or pager notifications, etc., all can help alerting the human operator. Saving these messages in a computer file is also helpful. In addition, electronic notification to an automated operator can also allow for automated data collection and time-stamping. Phone-home technologies have been used by IBM processors since 1981, and adopted by many manufacturers for storage array problem notifications. Many vendor products also allow for rapid notification to support personnel and management.

4) Action plan is created to solve the problem

   There are various means to create an action plan. Hopefully, the organization has action plans in "run books", and similar pre-planned and practiced processes to handle this "expected" emergency. (If the emergency represents a new kind of emergency, one would hope that a diagnosis and recovery process would be worked out and documented in an "update" to the run book!) But a key component of creating and employing this action plan is the existence of the diagnostic data. Else, you have to plan to obtain diagnostic data "on-the-fly". This has sometimes been referred to, unfortunately, as the "prayer meeting in front of the computer console". With poor planning, one has found that systems personnel can effectively "keep the system down", which is not their intent, as they try to diagnose a problem rather than use a pre-planned emergency action plan to capture diagnostic data and then get the system back up as soon as possible.

Probably one of the world's finest handling of an expected emergency was the ditching of the USAir airplane into the Hudson River in January 2009, when 155 lives were saved (Wald M. L., 2009). The pilot has repeated that "this is what he was trained to do", but his background and experience as an emergency situation educator, and as a glider pilot, plus extra hardware added to the plane to keep equipment electrically powered (emergency fan generator) when all engines were down, also helped (Altman, 2009). However this is the result of great engineering and great planning. It all looked so simple!

5) Problem solving starts. Data analysis can proceed rapidly with previously analyzed data, obtained and already digested by diagnostic tools. Raw data is fine, like a storage crash dump, but even that analysis can be sped up by a very smart diagnostic analyzer. Some crash-dump tools just format data, but others can give insight (Microsoft WinDbg ANALYZE) , and some can do a quick analysis of all system components and give a quick "state of the component" summary (z/OS IPCS ANALYZE verbs). This is not emphasized nearly enough, but a very smart storage dump analysis program can be very helpful. It can be very easy to get "lost" examining storage dumps, for even the most experienced problem-solvers, and some canned and pre-planned analysis is a wonderful head-start. Without some mechanical, pre-planned assistance in analyzing complex problems, the time can just disappear as one explores possibilities and potentially relevant data.

6) Problem solving ends

Eventually solving a problem on its first occurrence

I agree, speed in problem-solving is wonderful, but not all tools provide speed. Often, for airplane crashes, one expects the crash to get a definitive cause, effect and detailed explanation after a year, even though there are fantastic first fault tools involved (instrument data recorder and voice recorder). Data recorders are required to capture 88 key variables, but they often have the capability architecturally to record 1000 or more key variables. They capture a half-hour worth of data. The point is, even though science says that you eventually can solve a problem with a certain set of data, the engineering question we want to answer is, how to solve a problem rapidly, so we can get our computer systems back up and running fast, knowing that we have solved and prevented the next occurrence of this problem.

Software tool general classifications

I have developed a software problem-solving tool classification. I find it helpful when discussing products and comparing tools. I will use this classification later on.

Classification of Software Problem Solving Tools:

1) Level 1 – A tool that can determine if a software system is "up" or "down" – A binary single value (example: the "ping" command in TCP/IP network communications). It is relatively easy to determine if a server, or other computing entity, is operating sufficiently to respond to the query, "are you up?" There are many software tools that do this and they provide value in understanding if any critical components are not operating in a data-center.

2) Level 2 – A Level 2 Software tool provides data that is sufficient to match the current problem to a previously occurring already-diagnosed problem. This kind of tools provides, as a minimum, a summary description of problem – its symptom, "problem signature", or "characteristic" key values of critical data areas. There are many tools that facilitate matching of the current problem to others in a database.

3) Level 3- A Level 3 software tool provides all the data that is necessary and sufficient to solve a unique new problem. This is very difficult, and there is no one tool or system that is sufficient to perform at "level 3" capability for any and all problems, not yet,

perhaps not ever. But there are tools that can perform at "level 3" for particular environments or particular problems.

One could compare the volumes of data produced by these different software tools levels.

Level 1 tools produce a single binary value – 0 (down) or 1 (up)

Level 2 tools produce perhaps several kilobytes of data to describe the problem's signature.

Level 3 tools can provide several orders of magnitude, much more data, to sufficiently solve a complex system problem. If a complete storage dump, it could range into many gigabytes.

So, the size of these data collections ranges from 1 bit (level 1) to perhaps 4K-12K (several thousands) to 1 to 1000 gigabytes (thousands of billions).

Serviceability rating (SR)

As a measurement of the overall effectiveness of problem solving ability at your site, or in your product, I propose a quantity I call the "serviceability rating" (SR). The serviceability rating is the number of times a problem occurs, including the last time it occurs, which is when it is solved. A perfect **SR** is "1", indicating you solve every problem the first time it occurs;

"1" is also the lowest value attainable for the "**SR**". The maximum value? Well, it could be very large, but the primary benefit of computing the **SR** is for use in comparisons. A perfect score in the game of golf is "18"(18 holes-in-one), but this is not a practical measure, either ("18" is also the lowest numerical value in that game, too!). But even though no one reaches perfection in golf, the score is useful to compare one golfer to another, one golfer's golf game to another game he plays, and so forth.

What is the actual value of the **SR** in your environment? Hopefully, whatever it is, it will shrink closer to "1", after you apply the thinking you have learned in this book. **SR** may not be easy to determine, because if your organization is successful in self-service problem solving, you won't have a problem management system record (an incident report) that tracks that successful event. It might take a special study to determine what your **SR** is. In any case, it is useful to think of the **SR** as an overall measurement, a management tool, to evaluate this key aspect of your problem solving capabilities.

Serviceability percentage (SP)

The serviceability percentage (SP) is designed to easily manage and measure your success in solving problems on the first occurrence. You simply take the reciprocal of your **SR** and then multiply by 100. Thus:

SP = 1 / SR x 100

The **SP**'s value ranges between 0 and 100. If you solved all problems on their first occurrence (your **SR** is "1"), your **SP** would 1/1 x 100, which equals 100. If you solved problems on the second occurrence, then your **SR** is 2, and your **SP** is 1 / 2 x 100= 50. If half of your problems are solved on the first occurrence, and half on the second occurrence, then your **SP** is 1 / 1.5 x 100 = 67. Thus, your **SP** is a number between 0 and 100. As you improve your ability to solve problems on fewer and fewer occurrences, your **SP** will rise, approaching 100. It is easy to graph, and easy to measure improvements.

Serviceability time (ST)

The serviceability time is the average amount of time it takes to solve a problem. This would measure the time between when the problem occurs, and when the responsible user reporting it indicates that it is solved to his satisfaction. Obviously, we want **ST** to be as low as possible.

The *average* American family has 2.3 children ...
... but *none* of them have 2.3 children...

Yes, you are right, after introducing quality measures that use averages, I now disparage them! Well, all measures and statistics have their value and limitations. Besides measuring the overall quality of your organization and products by averages, you should be aware of extreme values, and most frequent values. The extreme values can be the most worrisome: what is the *longest* time it has taken to solve a problem? Is this a critical, visible, very important problem?

Also, are there any problems that occur very *frequently*? These too, are problems that require attention and resolution, and every effort that succeeds in reducing elapsed time for these (unavoidable?) problems has a large effect in improving overall measures, like serviceability time (**ST**), and serviceability percent (**SP**).

Collecting data to solve problems

We have some basic choices. To solve a problem, we could capture all of storage, for every instruction that a CPU executes. Impractical? Yes! Although, with a powerful hypervisor and a minimal performance requirement, you could capture quite a bit of data. You still can use a final system storage dump (UNIX crash, Microsoft crash, or mainframe SVC Dump or standalone dump).

...tracing

Performance data samplers are powerful and should be used extensively – besides displaying immediate data values, there should be a means of recording the history of key data values. We will further discuss performance monitoring and tools in the next chapter.

A technique used to solve many computer problems involves "tracing", where, like leaving bread-crumbs while walking through the forest, one indicates, for every change of direction (execution- switching and work-dispatching from one program to another), the position (computer location counter/instruction counter), some key register values, a time stamp, and other useful values. In addition to synchronous changes of processor control, asynchronous events like I/O interrupts from attached devices, external interrupts from timers and signals from other CPUs in the configuration, and special events (hardware tracing, for example) can be recorded. Actually, the asynchronous events, like I/O interrupts, are key, since they also drive changes of control processing. The main point is being able, at a micro level, to record changes in the flow of programs from one dispatchable unit of work of one system or application program, to another.

This has been used by IBM mainframes since the 1960's. In the past they have used special hardware assists to speed-up and provide other assists in the recording of data. Like airplane data recorders, there is only a fixed amount of memory devoted to the in-storage trace, so one cannot go all the way back in time (to when the system or application was initialized). When a problem occurs, and a user or system dump is captured, the trace table is included. Trace tables are very helpful, but they are not always sufficient alone to solve a problem. One surely makes their trace table as large as possible, to go back in time as far as possible.

I have also used "application" trace tables, which similarly capture key activities in a finite storage area and they are saved (captured) at the time of an error.

Traces are valuable, and have been implemented as powerful problem-solving tools, in many forms. IBM mainframe z/OS operating systems also have "Component Traces" to trace the flow of processing within various component parts of the larger operating system. These Component Traces trace normal operations synchronously, but can be modified to capture special data for expanded use as a second failure problem recreation tool.

I really want to emphasize the use of traces *concurrently* with normal operation, since they provide valuable diagnostic information at the time of a problem. Traces can give you very valuable first fault problem solving information. I have often seen traces used as second-fault problem solving tools, but with a judicious selection of parameters, they could be set up as first fault problem solving tools.

In the next chapter, we will use our knowledge of fault types, tool characteristics, and desired performance and other measurements to examine software service tools.

CHAPTER 5 SOFTWARE SERVICE TOOLS

"We shall not fail or falter; we shall not weaken or tire...Give us the tools and we will finish the job.

"Sir Winston Churchill (1874 - 1965),
BBC radio broadcast, Feb 9, 1941

We have already discussed the benefits of first fault problem solving techniques and concepts, and described some of the kinds of problems found generally in computer systems. We have also described some of the requirements and restrictions on various tools. In this chapter, we will spend some time in-depth describing many **built-in** tools, by category, and will point out advantages and requirements for each.

After concluding this chapter, you will, as a user, system administrator, manager, or designer, have a good expectation of the kinds of standard software tools to expect in any computer system. You will be able to utilize, to the fullest, the first-fault problem solving capabilities of the system you are given, without purchasing or developing additional tools. As a designer, you will have a better appreciation of the value of first fault software problem solving tools, and be able to help choose the best ones for your new products and their operating environments.

Messages

The capability of a software product to detect an error condition, and write an explanatory message to the user, is one of the most fundamental, and perhaps one of the least appreciated features, for first fault software problem solving. Originally designed for viewing by human computer operators, or programmers, in the case of an application program, nowadays, many messages are seen by automated operators – other computer programs. The best messages have searchable message prefixes, like an eight-character code (more details in the chapter on creating first fault facilities). These codes are powerful because they can be used to search databases, as well as the internet.

There are commercial products that focus on messages for analysis of system behavior (to be described in the section on commercial tools), Loglogic, and Log Rhythm.

Example of a message with a prefix: (from the IBM message manual):

```
IOS000I  IOS1000I   devn,chp,err,cmd,stat,[sens], [dcbblkct
| op**term | cylntrck], [ser], [jobname][,sens][,text]
```

Explanation: "The system found a permanent I/O error in device error recovery..." but there are more details to note.

The first is the message identifier, **IOS000I**. IBM uses a distinct format: a three character alphabetic identifier (here, "**IOS**"), followed by a 3-digit message number (here "**000**"), followed by a message suffix (here "**I**"). The IOS alphabetic component identifies the message as emanating from the "IOS" (I/O Supervisor) component, while the 3 digits are arbitrary, but always fixed for the message with this meaning, and the "I" is an indicator of the importance and action to be taken upon receiving the message ("I" is informational, no action really required; "A" means "action is required"; "W" is a warning of a major problem like a failing hardware part, and "E" indicates an operator intervention is required).

The details of IBM's coding/architecture system for messages is not important here, but just the value of the facts that:

- IBM has a specific architecture, a fixed format (even with variable parts) that all its messages follow.
- IBM's messages include a message identifier, which, alone, is a powerful search argument in IBM's manuals, IBM databases, in other vendor databases, or generally through the internet across multiple databases.

Problem Data Collector

Many vendors supply a script, or a program to collect data. The command or program is intended to be run as soon as feasible after the error has been experienced. The command collects a variety of data and packages it, often in a compressed format, for upload to the vendor support organization. The data collected will often include: key configuration files, the output of key status-interrogating commands, and various files of diagnostic information, which can themselves include message logs, error logs, and the like. Usually also included is a detailed listing of the system level (version and release numbers) and levels of the component program packages. Examples of this are: SUN Microsystems' **explorer** command and **Gather Debug Data** command suite (SUN Microsystems, 2009) and IBM AIX's **snap** command.

I have also used a Linux data collector script that was listed in a book (Wilding & Behman, 2006), similar to **snap** or **explorer**.

The commands are valuable, uniformly collecting a pre-defined large body of data, which would be very difficult to run manually. The sequence of commands are run near-simultaneously, much closer together than a human could run by entering the commands manually.

However, the data so gathered, for some problems, may not be gathered as close to the problem occurrence as possible. I like to compare problem data-gathering to the camera used in a photo-finish race. For my money, **snap** and **explorer** effectively take the photo-finish picture at best, a "few seconds" after the two leading horses have crossed the finish line. It is far better than nothing, and often very useful, but it has its limitations. A better picture would be taken immediately as the winner is crossing the finish line, in fractions of a millisecond, not seconds.

Also, the commands are designed to be run manually, not automatically. A human operator has to make the decision to run the command, although running the commands to gather the data could be automated creatively, but even if submitted automatically, the design of the command strings takes a lot of time to execute the script after the error has occurred, been detected, and the decision was made to collect data.

The data collected this way, I maintain, would surely qualify it for a rating as a "Level-2" first fault tool – in other words, it likely can be used to match the current problem to a previously known problem. The data so gathered could be used as a starting point for additional analysis – for problem reproduction, etc. But the data so gathered may not always be sufficient to find the failing sequence of instructions that caused the problem (whatever event caused **snap** or **explorer** to be run).

One valuable use of this standard vendor data-collector is to take a steady-state picture of a system. You could run the data collector when you first boot the system, and then you have a great comparison over time. Save this picture at the start of a test or production cycle. After you bring up the system, and get a layout of how virtual storage is allocated, and after you are ready to bring down the system after a long production run: take a snapshot then, and see if virtual storage goes back to its original allocation – if it doesn't, you have a memory leak. Before and after comparisons can be a very useful tool in your monitoring of production system health. Of course, you could also repeatedly run the scripts once a day, once an hour, etc, to get a greater number of comparison points.

I know of only one system that dynamically gathers significant diagnostic data at the time or an error, nearly simultaneously, and that is IBM's mainframe z/OS. Yes, Windows, UNIX and other systems take storage dumps, but z/OS captures a great deal of volatile data at the time of the error, and it is done dynamically and non-destructively: z/OS can take system virtual dumps and continue processing. This feature has been consistently and repeatedly re-engineered in succeeding version of z/OS to provide the least disruption while capturing the most significant problem-solving data: the feature is called the "SUMDUMP". For many instances, a z/OS crash dump captured dynamically can be a Level-3 category tool, but not always, unfortunately. Other systems have yet to do this instruction-level comprehensive data-capture automatically. We shall make additional similar comparisons among systems.

Version number, rev number or "About"...

Surely the one piece of data which is usually less than a line of data, eighty characters or less, is the product version level, more popularly called the "rev number" (product revision number). This is an incredibly useful piece of data that is very compact, and it refers to the "version number", the extent of program functionality (ideally, adding fix or modification-level to rev-level data would make this data set complete) and also the set of problems experienced and solved already at that rev level. Very often personal computer systems refer to this level information as the "About" information.

First symptoms of soft errors

Sometimes a "soft error" occurs. That would be a condition where a problem was recovered in some fashion, and no action needs to be taken immediately, but a "for your information" notification is made for future reference. Sometimes, systems (like humans!) have threshold standards which, when reached or exceeded, cause an action to be taken.

Thus, in the case of soft errors, we are truly concerned with the first occurrence of a fault (it is not a major destructive error occurrence, but it could lead to one.

"Black box" data recorders – traces

Generalized instruction-flow tracing

Yes, the term comes from the technology used in airplanes. Recent studies have proactively used data captured from airplane black boxes (Wald M. , 2007). In the case of computers, a "trace" monitors the flow of processing, at various levels (high, and very low). We will first talk about the very lowest level trace, as described by the IBM mainframe z/OS **system trace**.

Low level traces are found in mainframe systems, where changes in instruction flow are captured in the z/OS trace buffer. Essentially, mainframe traces capture the start of work, work (program) interruptions (I/O and timer and other processor) interruptions, and special events, like a hardware or program error (invalid operation code, store into protected area, etc). The general intent is to capture each start of a new program, when and why that work gets interrupted, each with key information about the instruction flow (location counter, privileged/user state, interrupt enablement, and others). You want to know where you are when each change of instruction flow occurs: call it a value, a vector (with position, direction and detailed state data).

Again, I compare the z/OS system trace to leaving bread crumbs as you traverse a route in the forest. With a fixed number of bread crumbs, you can space the bread crumbs wide apart to get further coverage. But, it's harder to see those crumbs if you are standing next to one crumb, and the next is five miles away! Thus, density is important – frequent traces are better, but consume more resources.

Of course, the number of bread crumbs corresponds to the size of your trace table. One could ask, "How large should I make my trace table?" And the best answer, without knowing any better, is that the larger physically tolerable, the better it is – the more likely if a crash occurs, the failing instruction sequence would be captured in that trace table.

Some of the more detailed commercial trace products boast the ability to replay a problem. This has been seen in some specialized products, and the ability to both visualize the problem, and slowly examine each step of a doomed process is very valuable. However, this hasn't been seen as a part of an individual operating system. Not yet!

Higher-Level, Application-Level and Component-Level Traces

I have used application-level traces: the thinking is similar. Keep a running record of where you've been, in case you have a failure and you wonder "how did I get *here*?"

Trace facilities are very valuable in software products. As a minimum, a trace should be available to be used as a "second fault" tool (turn on the trace when you have to recreate the problem). But if there is a well-engineered level of data collection and granularity, then some of these second-fault traces could be used as first-fault traces. Those are the best kind!

IBM z/OS Component Trace

A very strong example of a trace facility, actually a set of related, but different trace facilities, is the family of specialized traces in IBM mainframe z/OS, called Component Trace (IBM Corporation, 2008). IBM describes their family of tools as a continuous trace, useful for (my terminology) first- and second- fault problem resolution, or in just determining the status of a particular component (of the z/OS operating system). As of January 2009, there were currently 21 different components that had separately adjustable traces.

They can all run concurrently, and as a matter of fact, some do run with a default set of parameters, on-going, during normal production operation (thus they are "first-fault" problem resolution tools). Typically, the trace data is obtained by customer systems programmers/administrators, and used by the IBM support center, but its contents can and should also be viewed by the z/OS customer system administrator. I comment on this in our chapter of advice for users.

Storage dumps

One of the most important kinds of problem-solving tools, generally available in most operating system environments, is the storage dump. Most users would not consider this a user-friendly form of documentation, and indeed it is not. But a storage dump describes what has just happened inside your system. They come in great varieties, to the delight of the true aficionado of binary data! Storage dumps should be saved, when documentation suggests this (and it should) for analysis by the vendor support organization. Storage dumps come in at least these varieties, with various features:

- System storage dumps (often called crash dumps) vs. user dumps (also called core dumps or ABEND dumps)

- Complete or partial (is the whole system state contained in the dump, or just one user, or some other subset)?

- Formatted or unformatted (some data structures mapped out and listed as to the name of the location on the data structure *and* its value?), or, just the raw numerical storage contents?

- Intelligent formatting, or just listing field values with the names of the field in the data structure? Is there analysis of the *meaning* of the data, or is data displayed, in an easier format, rather than hexadecimal, octal, binary, or something similar?

- Automatically captured by the system, or captured by a user or system administrator in response to a command? Dumps captured automatically should have data which is less likely to be over-written. SUN Solaris and IBM z/OS have facilities to request a system dump by the computer operator such that the dump is captured dynamically, with no destructive effect to the running system.

- Is volatile data preserved for later re-use? The actual process of collecting a dump could overlay valuable data that you would want preserved. Does your system have a means of preserving a portion of volatile data before the dump process starts? Preserving volatile data is a feature of the IBM mainframe z/OS SVC Dump (a System Dump initiated automatically by "recovery routines").

- Is the dump synchronous, or asynchronous? Is it captured immediately, or is the data captured sometime after the error has occurred? The best results are from dumps captured immediately, synchronous with the occurrence of the problem.

Is it possible to have an operating system (a "control program", as they are sometimes elegantly called) which does not have a storage dumping facility? Yes. I worked with one such system in an environment where the software was really the microcode, the firmware for a product, but there was no facility until some time after its initial release, to dump and format the unit's processor storage – computer memory.

I have also worked with operating systems that needed major improvements in their data capture and storage dumping facilities. They eventually did get their needed improvements. This is all part of the story of continuous serviceability improvements. If you find you need it, implement it! And, for sure, you will find you need effective storage dumping facilities.

In any case, most operating systems and operating environments have storage dump functionality: dumps are valuable to the people at the highest level of technical support. If you are a user you should know which dumps to preserve, and how to save them for use by support. System administrators should surely be aware of storage dumps and how to ensure that they and their users capture them properly, and how to send them to the support organization.

Performance Monitors

Many systems have built-in performance monitors. At a minimum, you want to know the percent of available time-shared machine cycles are being utilized for: CPU, I/O devices (also pathways - channels or I/O cards), network, and storage. Often, graphic charts are helpful in viewing allocation of resources.

Besides "real-time" information, it is advantageous to be able to store in a file, if not all data, but at least accumulated averages of consumption, perhaps hourly CPU usage, and hourly device utilization, so as to be able to assess capacity. Additionally, you want to be able to prevent reaching a condition of over-consumption without a means of back-tracking to find out what component part of the workload reached saturation, and when.

In addition, if you are conducting a forensic analysis (problem-solving) of a critical performance problem, you need to be able to look backwards to see the interplay of work leading up to the problem: this file of data is invaluable.

Some performance monitors will cleverly show you by kinds of work, what resources each uses. The earliest forms of performance monitors will show you resources and their utilization. When you examine the view by each piece of work, you can see just what resources some specific work is waiting on, and you learn that if you increased or re-allocated that resource, you can speed up the processing of your work. Mainframe z/OS Resource Monitoring Facility (RMF) has a feature called the Work Delay Monitor, also known as Monitor III, which performs this functionality, for example.

Other performance monitors called "hot-spot" monitors, like Compuware's STROBE (Compuware Corporation) will tell you detailed, microscopic information regarding what parts of a program use a CPU most heavily. This can be used to tune a program, or redesign it for improved performance. Hot-spot analyzers perform sampling of performance WITHIN a program, at regular intervals.

Generally the hot-spot analyzers are really second-fault problem tools: You run the hot-spot analyzer on a particular application program after you determine that this application group is eating up a lot of CPU cycles.

Surely performance monitors, with real-time data, as well as accumulated and filed data will help solve a reported performance problem. This is a particular kind of instrument, for particular (performance) problems.

Error Records

Many operating systems now record various errors in a file. A quick scan of these files provides a great overall view of hardware and software problems experienced (and recovered?) by your system, and surely some of them will help you solve a problem to its root cause. Operating systems producing these now include Microsoft Windows/VISTA, with a hardware and software log, AIX and other Unix variants with an error report ("errpt" command), and IBM z/OS and z/VM (data is formatted by EREP – the error record formatting program). z/OS software error reports have been available since 1973, and hardware error reporting was performed even earlier.

Symptom-Solution Databases

They usually don't come directly with an operating system or application program environment, but access to vendor databases with searchable lists of known problems as well as the associated fixes for them is an incredibly valuable tool. It allows for user self-service. Some vendors, like Microsoft, have made great strides in first-fault software problem resolution, by allowing a user PC's Microsoft XP and VISTA, to name two examples, to automatically upload a symptom string to Microsoft's database at its website, and scan for a problem and associated solution matching the user's current problem, and then notify the user of the result of the search (a match, with a description of the problem and solution, or no match found). This is incredibly powerful, and often succeeds in automatically downloading a usable description of a fix to be displayed to the user. This is truly impressive.

Can the success of this be improved? Absolutely, it can. One wonders what the overall statistics are, and expect that the ability to match a customer's problems to an already-solved problem does not yield 100% success. I have ideas (see later chapter) on how this matching can be performed better.

In other environments, one has to manually search the vendor database (or the vendor does the search), comparing various symptoms (which symptom is most important) to the list of recorded symptoms. Obviously, this is the very definition of a Level-2 first fault tool – being able to use the tool to compare a current problem with a history of known problems.

Not to be under-estimated, is the wide-open use of Google or Yahoo or other generalized web-searches, in seeking a match between a problem symptom with a known problem and solution. Many vendor problem-solution records are available by use of those global web-searches also.

Whether done manually by a user or system administrator, or automatically by your system, the problem database is an invaluable problem-solving tool. It takes some experience and knowledge of the details of each search method and options, to get the best results. Often, it is very valuable to do searching yourself, and be able to mention the searches you've attempted, and the results you've obtained when contacting a vendor for their support (see more in the advice to Users chapter).

These same databases often have varieties of FAQ (Frequently Asked Questions) and best practice (what experience has shown to be the best way to use the product). These database articles could be hit when searching "symptom strings", and they are valuable too.

Automation Tools

Many systems have various features to speed up various parts of the first fault problem resolution process.

Generally, various systems have script and/or command generation methods that can be useful for specifying data-gathering commands when detecting a problem. These tools can be useful in notifying users and management of the problem also.

Systems that collect problem data automatically are even better. This is often the case with system (crash) and user (core/ABEND) storage dumps, but sometimes particular dumps, or dumps tailored for particular errors are necessary. The z/OS SLIP command collects customized data for specified error types and environmental conditions (Siewiorek & Swarz, 1998).

Phone-home and internet-connected notification

Phone-home, via telephone, or via internet, can be very valuable in directly notifying support organizations rapidly to immediately start problem-solving activities. Right now, it tends to be most appropriate for the Enterprise level, in major data-centers, but the example of the automobile companies (On-Star by GM is the most prominent example), indicates that phone-home and automatic problem notification for individual users is appreciated (10,000 ON-STAR notifications due to accidents – crashes).

PHONE-HOME TECHNOLOGIES - A detailed look

Phone-home was originally developed to report hardware problems. An early implementer was IBM, in 1981, with its 3081 server and its entire 308X server family. Hardware problems were reported via automated dial-out with a modem, through a telephone, to a headquarters system for logging, diagnosis, notification to hardware repair people of the location of the failing unit, as well as call-out of the required spare parts those repair people would be picking up on their way to the site of the failing machine. This expedited repair, and it greatly facilitated headquarter detailed knowledge of the install base, including soft as well as hard errors.

There is fantastic opportunity for "data mining" - drawing relationships among failing systems, and reliable vs. unreliable parts - with all this control over the detailed automated machine-readable real-time status of all the hardware installed by a vendor, world-wide. These techniques were quickly employed by other server hardware vendors and also makers of storage arrays, such as EMC, STK, and SUN Microsystems, and the former Encore Computer . Many other companies use these technologies, including industries outside the Information Technology industry.

The opportunity still exists for further exploitation of phone-home for monitoring *software* problems and system failures, with similar automated analysis and reporting to service personnel for the vendor and customer. Full control of applications and systems software is now possible, but perhaps has not been exploited nearly to the extent of hardware monitoring.

One should note that some systems that allow phone-homes out to the vendor also allow the vendor to "dial-in" for further detailed analysis. One can envision that whether analysis is all automated or part automation and part manual analysis by engineers dialing-in, the total effect is very powerful for problem resolution. One should design a system with as much automation as possible, but allowing manual dial-in to fill in any deficits of automation. One should plan to think to take frequently-performed manual procedures that are done via dial-in, into automated processes that can be performed automatically. It is also very powerful to compare, in real-time, the results of dial-in data collection to established headquarters install bases of parts histories, problem symptoms, and other information.

Software fault-detection systems can notify users of a problem, but an integrated analysis (symptom matching through a database upstream at the vendor site), has not been exploited nearly as fully as possible. Microsoft has made a good start with matching of its symptom string (minidump) of Windows problems, to matchups with known problems and associated solutions.

Microsoft's Automatic Problem-Solving In The Cloud

Microsoft has done some very promising use of error handling via databases "in the cloud" (accessible by users automatically through the internet), described with the Windows Error Reporting functionality (Microsoft Corporation, 2009). The interface in Windows Error Reporting allows matching of system problems to its own Windows database, but also has a capability for classifying symptoms in "buckets", by initial error description, both for system errors (stop codes), and for user errors.

The symptoms, or error descriptions, include the module that experienced the error and offset into the module   that is very specific. Also included are modules currently loaded, and module and hardware version numbers, and other information.

Microsoft allows notification of other third-party vendors who collaborate with them to be notified of errors in their products. The user is signaled if there is a match to a known problem and solution, or not. It is a great start, and provides an integrated framework for the participating third-party software vendors.

I expect to see more automation tools for first-fault problem solving in the near future, and phone-home is a major component of this technology.

CHAPTER 6 WHAT USERS CAN AND SHOULD DO

"People often say that motivation doesn't last. Well, neither does bathing—that's why we recommend it daily."

Zig Ziglar

s

We will be talking about two kinds of users: the general users of a computer system: those sitting in front of their PC or workstation, as well as the system administrators, the technical people who set up the systems. The primary audience is the general users, actually. But the system administrators/system programmers also need to understand how to set things up to make life better for the general users, regarding first fault software problem solving.

Let me follow the advice in Seven Habits of Highly Effective People (Covey, 1989), and start with the end, the goal, first: Your goal, as a user, is to be able to initiate a problem resolution session with your support organization, and be understood as an intelligent, informed and constructive user who has worked sensibly and done everything possible to be able to articulate your problem.

My goal, when I am the end-user, is to have already collected the data that the vendor has told me he requires to solve the problem – I usually collect more information in case that would be helpful. I often examine the data first before I report the problem to the vendor. My goal is to be as complete as possible, such that the vendors never have to ask me to recreate the problem to get diagnostic data.

I convey the data to the vendor. I treat the engagement as a sales presentation, where I must sell myself as a competent person who deserves to be served, who should not be sent to the back of line due to incorrect or insufficient problem data. I have found this works very well in getting the attention of support organizations and getting the assistance I require to get my issue resolved. You can do this too, and reap similar benefits.

To be successful you should:

Prepare before you use the product in "production"

- Read product service and support instructions carefully, before you experience any problems
- Go through a dry-run, if possible, sending a problem description, with all required data, to the vendor
- Follow vendor best practices in their associated documents that come with the product or are available on-line. Be able to point to how well

you follow the vendor advice if you have to speak to their support organization.

- Obtain the very latest in data-gatherer products, and resolve to always get the vendor's latest data-gatherer product and install it, as updates become available.
- Try searching through the vendor's database(s) and performing general internet searches, to see what kinds of information may be generally available, in case your problem is indeed with their product.
- Check with your representative in your organization's system administration department to see if they have any particular requests regarding support.
- Volunteer, whenever possible, when new releases of the product are made available for early user testing by the system administrators at your site. You can get more support and advice this way.

When you have a production problem

- Gather at least the minimum data required by the vendor.
- Gather more data if you feel it could help.
- Probably the single most valuable piece of data you should be sure to have is the product version and release number. Often this is maybe three or four characters of data, but it is very helpful in pointing out level of the functionality. Indirectly, it points successfully to a subset of the known problems for your product – the problems already discovered for that product rev-level.
- Examine the data, and earnestly try to solve the problem through vendor symptom-problem database and web searches, if you have any time available and the problem is not yet critical to your site. Record the results of your search: be able to tell the (vendor) support organization about the results of your due diligence.
- Keep a thorough audit trail, as much as possible, regarding what you did (Agans). Support organizations will ask you the steps you took, so you should be ready to recount what you saw, what you did, and what changes you made. If you can have a written account of this prepared, you can go over the steps you took to gain further insight before you call the support organization. There are a few tools available, discussed later, to help automate the collecting of the steps you took
- Then, report the problem to the (vendor) support organization.
- If the support organization asks you to re-create the problem, be sure to ask what tools you should use to gather more data so the problem

can be resolved next time. Also, ask for them to try to recreate the problem in their lab, if they don't immediately offer this. I was once asked, when I was in the service department for a company, working on a problem that the "product support group" couldn't yet solve, to wait until the problem reoccurred at the customer site. My urgent question was "what *additional* data should I collect the next time it occurred so *you* will be able to *solve the* problem?" You will find this question *est*ablishes a true partnership with your support partners.

- As a last resort, if there is an urgent problem that you need to report and you know you have the barest minimum of diagnostic information, I would advise you to confess this honestly to the support organization up front. Then provide what explanation you can. This is helpful.

A prepared user will succeed in getting the best results from his support organization. If you make note of the above steps and follow them you will get far better results from your support organizations. The next chapter will help your organization plan for creating their own first fault software problem resolution product service facilities.

CHAPTER 7 CREATING SOFTWARE WITH FIRST FAULT PROBLEM SOLVING CAPABILITY

"Imagination is the beginning of creation. You imagine what you desire, you will what you imagine and at last you create what you will."

George Bernard Shaw (1856 - 1950)

If you are reading this chapter, then you are a software engineer or software developer, a manager of developers, a tester, field or customer support or help desk person, or just a user with deep curiosity, or anyone else with a need to know just how to create software products with first fault problem-solving characteristics. Adding this capability to software is not difficult: all that's required is an understanding of collecting data, and a willingness to continuously improve your software.

Now that you truly understand the value of first-fault problem solving, and you are aware of the variety of tools provided with systems, and what kinds of tools are generally used to be successful, I'm guessing you are highly motivated to use these techniques in the new application or the new operating system you will be creating. Am I right? I hope so! But *how*, and *where* do you start? And how do you create facilities to solve problems that you never had before? Read on.

Defensive Programming, and being even more defensive than *that*

It is helpful to be familiar with an excellent practice called "defensive programming" (Goodliffe, 2007). Defensive programming was just mentioned earlier in this book. Historically, it is a very early "best practice" in computer programming, but I want you to think of this as a starting point in the development of your first-fault software problem-solving mindset. It is a great "best practice", and an excellent foundation to create software that can solve a problem when it first occurs.

I think of defensive programming as analogous to "defensive driving", and that would help you if the term is not yet very familiar. When you drive defensively, you assume that the other drivers are *not* careful. You must be careful yourself: you must give yourself extra room on the road to make emergency maneuvers. You assume other drivers may ignore red lights and stop signs; therefore you look both ways and are ready to stop when you approach intersections. You anticipate problem areas up ahead – dense traffic, impaired visibility, and other potential impediments. In any case, you devote a lot of time, energy, and resources to the infrequent and unlikely event that you will encounter a dangerous situation.

Similarly, people programming defensively routinely take steps such as checking return codes, providing for recovery of errors, and allowing programs to be restartable without a reboot. And, they test their input data, before using it. They assume that errors can occur from other sources, and they must prepare for them.

If you were to drive according to the first fault problem solving methods, and if your environment was optimized, you would have these additional features:

- An automotive "black box" in your vehicle.
- Monitoring and accessibility of the black box by the manufacturer, (think ONSTAR for General Motors vehicles).
- Video cameras, and they would be recording on all six sides of your vehicle (including sky-facing roof and road-facing cameras), providing you with six recordings of their video output. You would prefer to have intelligence built into the cameras, to focus on an object approaching your vehicle that appeared to be threatening. All this data would be recorded for purposes of first fault problem solving.

If your car, which you already drove defensively, had such first-fault problem solving equipment, is there any doubt you have significantly improved your potential for success in resolving automobile problems, including crashes?

Programming for first-fault problem solving is "defensive programming", but super-charged, accelerated. You can and should code defensively. The two mantras are:

DEFENSIVE PROGRAMMING: Errors can and will occur and you must prepare for them.

Vs.

FIRST FAULT SOFTWARE PROBLEM SOLVING capability: Errors can and will occur and you must be able to use the software such that the errors can be solved right after their first occurrence.

If you don't believe in *defensive programming*, then you surely will not believe in, nor value *first fault problem solving*. One might think that the cost of creating first fault problem-solving capability would be larger than the cost for defensive programming, but bear in mind there are significant benefits, including a potentially measurable return on investment, for defensive programming. One would expect, and in fact receive, even more benefits by programming for *first fault problem solving*.

Programming for first fault problem solving could be called **extreme defensive programming**, or **extremely defensive programming**, if you choose. When you choose to program so that you can solve a software problem the first time it occurs, you are worried, also, that an error may have occurred in your *own* program. It is a super-set of the philosophy in defensive programming.

You should still anticipate that errors could occur from other sources – the programs or services or functions that you invoke - and you should still program defensively. Thus, if one worries about errors occurring in external entities, and also internally within one's own space, then they surely have anticipated errors within the universe of where your program operates. You worry with the added incentive to solve problems that could occur with the data available right after they occur.

How can you solve a problem that has occurred within your program? Do you use something that is broken to fix itself? It is not as self-contradictory as it could seem. Much of your program does and will operate correctly; else it would never have been in production at all. To solve the problems within your program, you must anticipate a problem occurring.

Are you ready to proceed now?

Concepts

Each aspect of software development needs to participate in planning for first fault problem-solving: these include designers, developers, testers, and support organizations.

Designers

Designers, please consider the users. Make life easy for them to collect diagnostic data the first time the problem occurs. Automation is best, but an easy non-automated system or set of commands will work as well. Be sure the methods are documented in user manuals, online, in support documents, and anywhere else your system documentation is stored. Be aware of the behavior of your support organization. Do the engineers there routinely request that the problem be reproduced, without even trying to debug it with available data? Have you described what available data is?

You have a lot of choices of features for first fault problem solving: dumps, traces, scripts, error messaging, error codes, performance monitors.

Ensure the process continually improves itself. If a problem is not solved on its first occurrence, encourage support people to supply design improvement suggestions in their error reports. You should also examine the results of analysis to find out how many problems are *not* solved on their first occurrence, and resolve to create improvements: it would be nice if the support organization were driving you, but perhaps the behavioral change would have to start elsewhere. It behooves you to determine the cost of multiple service incidents and justify first-fault problem solving features as cost-reductions (go the extra mile and show how it could improve customer satisfaction and accelerate product acceptance).

Designers: it's an established fact that you are the creative ones, the ones who lead your product and services development organizations. But you'll ultimately save yourself and your organizations a great deal of time and effort, if you can fully exploit your colleagues' contributions and accept the fact that many of the best-conceived ideas for service tools and products come far from your position in the product development cycle. They come from field service people, and from function and systems testers, who are the first to use products, and are operating under real-time constraints when solving problems. Service tool ideas later come from customer system administrators, who support your product at their workplaces.

Serviceability and service tools are applications used by testers, support people and customers. Listen to them, and try to dig and discover the various service methods they have, and let them help you with the concepts, while you help to refine their "rude and crude" and "quick and dirty" ideas into strong, supportable products.

What is the absolute *minimum* set of software features required for a software operating system, or middle-ware, or application? The same kinds of tools, or does each layer of product require different kinds of tools? What minimum tools are required? It would be worthwhile to do some kind of comprehensive study of successful vs. unsuccessful software products, and determine the kinds of software tools in each, and from this study, come up with an empirical rule-of-thumb.

Additionally, think back to system "YUK". What features would provide minimal capabilities to improve debugging of software problems? What features would provide the basics for a good opportunity to solve problems on their *first* occurrence? What are the minimal features for System "YUK"? How closely does the system you are working with resemble system "YUK"?

What features does it have already, what needs to be improved, what can you schedule for further improvement while making significant small improvements now?

Personally, based on a career solving problems in the field, in escalation teams, and in product design, development and testing, and considering much thought, reflection, and analysis, I recommend the following features, which can be created all at once, or in successive stages:

REQUIRED: A storage dump capability where the whole address space is dumped for the operating system, middle-ware, and/or application.

MINIMUM ENHANCEMENTS: First, provide messaging and/or codes. Ideally, messages are well-architected for rapid use and effective searching. Next, be sure to create a storage dump formatter for the most important and most frequently analyzed data structures. Finally, a "data collector" program or script that a user could easily run to gather the most valuable diagnostic data.

SUPPLEMENTED: Concurrent trace (first fault problem solving), or minimally, a second-fault tracing tool that could be easily turned on to become a first fault problem solving tool.

ADDITIONAL ENHANCEMENTS: Enhancements to the storage dump formatter which performs intelligent analysis of the storage dump, regarding the "health" of important components and detailed descriptions of anomalies found, where the "blood tests" were found to be "outside normal ranges": an "ANALYZE" verb, as in Microsoft Windows (WinDbg) and z/OS (IPCS – Interactive Problem Control System). Error reporting (hardware AND software). Performance monitors, extensive second-fault tracing. Instruction-level traces (Intel x86 Debug Registers or IBM mainframe Program Event Recording), hypervisors for extensive tracing, etc.

- On-the-fly, field service people often create scripts and tools to debug products. They surely have to do this when they must tell a client to "recreate the problem". When service people and developers recreate problems, if they don't have a good "second fault" problem solving tool, they likely have coded at least one tool, script, or process to replicate the problem, *and* one other tool to collect sufficient diagnostic data to solve the problem. If those service people have created a new script, without further prodding, they may keep this hidden.

Even worse, they might discard the logic and software fragment. In any case, these are valuable thoughts that if not captured through a problem management system, or other immediate means, are essentially lost. You need ways to regularly recapture this. Help them bring their scaffolding and rudimentary products into full product features.

- Customers, too, may have ideas for serviceability tools and requirements for faster problem resolution. If your organization has an official user group, like IBM SHARE or GUIDE, HP-Ux's "Connect" user group, or some official regular user group meetings, be sure to encourage user groups to tell you their needs for service tools and features. Their requests could help justify improvements that would increase acceptance of products and improve customer loyalty. Be sure to consider publicizing the first fault problem solving improvements you design into your products. In any case, these serviceability suggestions can be valuable.

- Consider multiple different places in the code. Ask the question, "Can I service a problem if it occurs *here*"? There are more questions: "What would a storage dump look like if the system or application failed at *this* point, and generated a storage dump"? Also, "could our support organization solve the problem from the storage dump without any further information?"

- Do you need to add features to the product to aid serviceability? You may be working with the software developers on these issues, also. Ask these questions yourself as you create designs, and also in meetings: in design inspections (Fagan, 1976), or walkthroughs, or peer reviews, whatever your organization uses to apply the efforts of multiple people to team together to improve your code. This particular question should also come up in the minds of the development engineers and test engineers, who should be invited to participate in design reviews and inspections, as well as code reviews, and other development meetings. You do have a large audience of people analyzing your design, don't you? Testers should be encouraged to *think* about whether a problem in the code being inspected or examined by a walkthrough could be solved, and what could be used to solve it (Freedman & Weinberg, 1990).

- Create data-collector tools – script-type tools, minimally, to be run manually by a human script submitter after the problem occurs; optimally, these data collectors will run automatically right after the problem is detected.

- For systems software, or a product's internal firmware, I see a set of crash-dump generation, capture and formatting tools as a real bare minimum.

- Enhancing the bare minimum of tools for the system, middle-ware, or application: Besides storage dumps, a tool for tracing operations, to some level of detail, would be advantageous. This could be a tool to run the "next time" a problem occurs, a second-fault tool, but if it's possible to run concurrently on-the-fly without disrupting normal operations, then it would be even better, and it would be running as a first-fault problem resolution tool.

I prefer software with:

⇨ Messages, architected with message ids
⇨ Crash dump capability
⇨ Dynamic on-the-fly non-destructive system dumps and/or application dumps
⇨ Error reporting/logging
⇨ Concurrent traces (first-fault traces)
⇨ Extensive second-fault traces
⇨ Hardware-supported second fault trace capabilities.
⇨ An associated hypervisor for powerful test and test analysis capabilities.

As a designer of operating systems, middleware, or applications software, you need to assess the serviceability tools already present on your platform, and supplement product features as needed. Analyze experience reports from testing organizations, or, even better, from user organizations. Very often, people will create such a report, often right after a long-term project. They are often called post-mortems, experience reports, or lessons learned. Their value is immeasurable; however, unfortunately they are under-utilized, of that, I'm convinced. Sometimes these reports are written with a lot of emotion born out of frustration, but that articulated frustration can be very helpful in thinking of improvements that could have made the product more tolerable, and definitely need to be considered when creating successor products in the same corporate organization.

- You may have to dig the first time you do this, but you should specially examine a set of costly, difficult and/or unsolved problems, as a seed for future software service improvements. The goal is "continuous improvement", not "continual frustration"! Unsolved problems may be closed as "can not reproduce" or "abeyant", or other such indeterminate closing code. These also point to tools that are needed. It would be worthwhile to examine these problems. Why was this problem not solved? What data would have been useful to have on hand to solve this problem? Imagine what kind of tool would have been useful to have to capture the data to enable this problem to be solved, even if the tool cannot be created immediately. Put the idea into a long-term plan and accumulate all votes for future product/features. More or less votes could accelerate or decelerate the creation of the future service product, but even if in a long-term plan, just putting in a plan for it is a major step forward.

- Besides "unsolved" problems, your problem/incident database may include many problems that took a long time to solve (calendar time), or problems that took many numbers of occurrences or incidents to occur, including production incidents and/or test system problem reproduction attempts. Your database may also point to problems that have occurred frequently and took some time to solve: those occurrences also point to opportunities to employ "first fault software problem solving" benefits to reduce problem solving efforts – that is if you can't prevent the problem's occurrence! Analyzing the trends of frequently occurring or difficult-to-solve problems is valuable.

- Consider the problem-fix-FAQ database your organization will have on its website. User capabilities to perform self-service would help you greatly. A valuable feature of many problem-management systems is a means to help conversion of a completed problem report into a more readable and reusable "FAQ". And frequently-used "FAQ" documents may provide the basis for software serviceability improvements, in an effort to automate the symptoms and responses pointed out by the FAQ. Can you monitor the number of times a FAQ was used in problem-solving?

- Keep vigilant to build serviceability features into your product, rather than add those features on in some later phase. The future gets delayed easily, and building into a product is far easier than adding on. I've worked with systems that had messages, but they weren't architected, and they didn't have architected message identifiers; unarchitected messages without message identifiers are far more difficult to work with than those which have the message identifiers. It may be extra work to add message identifiers when you initially create the software, but it is well worth the effort. Experience has shown that the work of performing updates to make messages architected with message identifiers becomes very onerous to perform after a product is created.

    One could see that when you decide to revamp all of your messages, you cause almost all, maybe all of your modules to be "opened up" for changes, even if it just to place a message identifier at the front of a message string: You have to recompile the changes and surely you have to test that the message can be presented successfully as in the past. You also have to verify that the module's functionality has not been negatively impacted – that the module still works as before (regression test). Thus, just appending a message id in the front of messages becomes a major, potentially risky undertaking, causing significant rework for your whole product.

    Even if you are adding on to a system without architected messages, it could be worthwhile to use architected messages in the new component. Better to start somewhere, rather than leave the whole system with the non-architected messages.

- Make it easy for the user to obtain serviceability data (the minimum is that "data-gatherer"), and perform initial analysis himself. Be sure to include a "best practices" document, describing data required to raise a support issue, and how to get it, along with your standard print and online publications. A software service document (using tools, analyzing problems, reporting problems) would be a significant help.

- Strongly consider the value of remote access by internet, "phone-home", or "dial-in" capabilities for your product. The ability to have your company's engineers access a failing system reduces the need for external service ease-of-use features and provides real-time assistance. But some secure sites in particular industries (defense, banking, and others) will not allow phone-home or dial-in or internet access, even if it were to be secured, and thus ease of data collection is very important, not trivial and only for use by the unsophisticated: the military and banking are surely large sophisticated markets for your products.

- Exerciser-tools used by test organizations can be helpful for demonstrating or verifying performance, if they create a repeatable sustained load. A functionality verifier can also be used to verify correct product installation or successful upgrade – some are called IVPs – Installation Verification Programs. Be imaginative! Tools can be found all over and added to your arsenal. You may not have to add much to create a real product feature from a home-grown tool. It will not be difficult to "productize" something that works. Look around your organization, amongst, field service, technical support, and quality assurance/testing departments!

- Consider using / relying on a third-party tool, such as AppSight, or Precise Software (see the chapter on "Commercially-Available First Fault Software Service Tools"). Creating your own serviceability features should be more manageable and certainly cheaper. If you start out *depending* on other company's products, you could limit your options in the future. It is better to analyze your needs for product serviceability, create your own, and then, if needed, supplement your operations with third party products that add value. Other companies could drop products, raise their fees, fail to upgrade to newer required technologies; another software company could go out of business or be acquired. Keep your options open, as much as possible. And analyze your serviceability attainment and needs.

Developers

You will have to think differently. If you don't already, you will have to consider that others could find a problem, a defect in your code, and it actually is better that way. You are likely accustomed to being presented with a problem from a tester or a service organization. You will (almost automatically) tell them to re-create the problem, and then devise a code change to either write messages, force a crash, or perform some other function that we now call adding a "serviceability feature". Perhaps you refer to this as *instrumenting the code*. In preparing your code for first fault problem solving, you will now think: "How would I code it if *recreating the problem* was *not* an option?!" You should think in terms of making the code "self-instrumenting".

Here are some suggestions: create a block of data that would be consulted if there were a failure in your code. This can be called a "status block". We will use this term again. This block would contain the following:

- Character-string labels for this block, for easy visibility in a storage dump
- List and count of resources owned by this program
- The value of serialization indicators ("locks" held, global counters).
- Flags set on and off, indicating which external function or program have been invoked and is in progress.
- An indicator or set of indicators, regarding logical phases in this program. It would indicate what step in being performed in the current program. This could be done with bit-string "footprints", "phase-ids", or counters. This is a handy shortcut to help a person debugging this program determine what has happened already in the program. This technique is endorsed by IBM in guidance to developers writing recovery routines for third party software that runs on an MVS mainframe operating system (IBM Corporation, 1994). The technique is used for programs that will either recover failed processing, or enable the processing to be invoked again. All we are using the technique for is to determine logically where we are in processing at the time our program fails. We are not concerned with the added functionality of recovering from the error and moving on, as IBM and 3rd party developers perform with IBM's z/OS recovery routine design.

The bit-strings, phase-ids, and/or counters, in essence, serve as a trace of activity within a program. Thus, as z/OS uses this technique for every one of its internal programs, all programs can have a kind of a "trace table", which can appear in a storage dump. As a matter of fact, IBM's z/OS has required that all of its recovery routines have recovery routines of their own. Thus, this internal tracing, this "status block", is embedded within z/OS's own recovery routines, besides the mainline program it is protecting. This foot printing and detailed status block is a very powerful diagnostic facility.

• An embedded software designer, with experience in the space program, Steven Stolper, has written about a trace table design and methodology (Stolper, 2007). He makes the point that a trace table can be created globally, or locally, for individual programs or functions. This is a great idea – using a particular focused trace table for a sub-component of a larger program.

Think again – are you often asked to recreate problems, or instrument your product for the service organizations? How would you add code to capture that data automatically so you don't need to be called upon? Can you create data collection points in your program (sort of a serviceability checkpoint)?

Do you truly practice defensive programming? Do you check all return codes from programs or functions you invoke? How helpful are you REALLY when you get a non-zero return code? Do you practice ultra-defensive programming, to make your program's problems self-diagnosing?

Do you have architected messages?

Do you provide a special formatter for YOUR components in your organization's storage dump formatter?

Do you invite testers to your code walkthroughs and inspections? Invite them, and request that they hold test walkthroughs and invite you too.

Does your organization use serviceability "bug reports"? In other words, is it possible for a user or tester to create a defect report seeking an improvement in the functionality of your program to facilitate problem resolution? That category should be available to them.

Are you allowed to add code to improve serviceability, or would you have to fight your management to add features of this sort?

Testers

You should have great impact on your product's capability to provide data sufficient to debug a problem on its first occurrence. You, after all, are the first users of the product, and the very first support organization performing debugging and troubleshooting. Do you use your own product's serviceability tools to debug problems you find, or do you use special internal test-department-only monitoring and data-gathering tools? Do you request problem re-creation and scaffolding from developers when you find problems in their code? At some point in your testing process, you should free yourself from special internal-use-only tools and use the diagnostic tools the field uses to solve product problems. And you should view every time a developer needs to recreate a problem as an opportunity you should both investigate to make the software self-diagnosing.

Oh, by the way, does your organization use its own products in production, at the very highest "rev levels", before customers get those products? This too is essential to test the serviceability of your products. I once heard the argument, "oh, we can't use **XYZ** in production. **XYZ** is too problematic. We have a product to deliver to the world". Never mind that the organization's product *was* "**XYZ**"! Have you heard this argument, or seen its results? Let's hope you aren't the one saying this or even accepting this practice.

You should have a means of evaluating your product's serviceability tools and features. You should not be exclusively using scaffolding or test features that field customers and/or service organizations do not have, and if you do use special products to service the product, you should work with development to integrate those special features into the product that customers use.

It's been said before that "you should eat your own cooking". Often that is interpreted to just mean, running products that your company offers, but regarding serviceability, you must also think of using field service tools, and using them often. Too often testing organizations can find it easy to use home-grown tools that customers and field personnel do not have. "Testing serviceability" should be a key mission in your life. Is it?

Also, you should be able to evaluate additional service features provided to users (instructions, data-gatherers, best practices, etc). If YOU can't resolve your company's products on its first occurrences, then your customers won't be able to do that either.

Do you have good relationships and communications with the developers and their organization? You should. Developers should incorporate your ideas into their products. Help developers. Invite them to test inspections/walkthroughs to let them see what services you are performing for them.

Whether you are a member of an independent, "stand-alone" testing organization, or of another team within a smaller developer organization (Loveland, Miller, Shannon, & Prewitt, 2004), great relationships with developers will be a big help. The earlier you can help in the development process (assist the designers, if possible, too!), the more of an impact you can have and the easier it will be to add serviceability features.

Testing the serviceability of a product

Have you seen this done? Not just testing to see if the code operates without failing (Does the storage dump formatter run without crashing? Do messages print clearly without garbage characters?), but testing the *serviceability*, which should really mean, testing to see if the whole product's serviceability features are *usable and effective* for a problem-solver. Have you done serviceability testing to see if the product's first-fault serviceability tools really *work* as planned, to be effective for your company's field force and users (Myers, 2006)? It actually is rare, but the need for this will inevitably grow over time, as larger and larger install bases of easy-to-use smaller systems with lesser skilled general users will increase.

This author had an opportunity to perform such a serviceability evaluation of one tool within a product feature very early in his career, but didn't fully exploit the chance. A feature that was "commonly known" to be ineffective was to be evaluated. How I would have handled this golden opportunity differently today! In any case, management collected a group of workarounds the testing department used and forwarded it to the development organization as a list of likely useful functional improvements. Those workarounds were implemented in the product.

One concept, if you perform fault injection testing, would be to create the faults in such a way that evidence of the fault injector disappears from a storage dump. Then you could give the ensuing fault-generated problem documentation to a fellow tester, and see if they could use production diagnostic analysis tools to see if they could debug the fault so generated/simulated (Vostokov, Private correspondence with Dan Skwire regarding testing serviceability, 2009). This is an additional way to test the serviceability of your products.

Usually, I am accustomed to seeing organizations improve the serviceability of their products, by making incremental changes to products already released. But how about special testing, in-house, before the product is generally available, to see if the tools can help solve problems, and then, if necessary, changing the product's serviceability features to make them more effective, before general availability? How about an explicit "pilot test or a "field serviceability test"?

I have only seen this once, with the special case of the US Census Bureau for 2010, running a pilot test in 2006 (two major districts using the special purpose hardware and software) for a one-time only product, hand-held computers for address verification, in a 3 month planned trial, three years before the production date (January 2009). Of course, the Census bureau did have a long-term goal: it is not a commercial enterprise that is in any hurry to get a product to the market, so one could argue that the Census bureau had a luxury that others don't have. Still, there is considerable value in performing a serviceability pilot test, if you can. Don't you agree?

In the Census Bureau pilot test, some problems were found and improvements made: Two new serviceability features were added: A special reset for a currently active and jammed or looping application, and a "synchronize" function to force a send/receive to the headquarters server when a unit was in a service mode being analyzed. The features were added after experience from the pilot test was analyzed. Additionally, an updated assessment of the proper sizing of the HELP desk organization was performed (make it much larger!).

The pilot program is an excellent idea, and sure is a production-similar method to evaluate service tools and processes. Some organizations will call a *pilot* test a *beta test*, or some similar concept. Usually, focus is placed on the reliability or usability of the main features of the product, but paying attention to serviceability success with the product's prescribed service tools and processes will be very valuable.

Management

Finally some advice to the managers of software development and user organizations: Whether you are a manager of designers, developers, testers, service organizations, or just end-users, you have the same problem: how do I change the mind-set of people doing problem-solving the "same old way": hearing that a problem has occurred, adding temporary serviceability code or scaffolding, and then reproducing problems?

You ask yourself, "How do I change my organization to *think* differently, to *think* of solving the problem on its first occurrence, to actually succeed in changing their thinking and their products so this *does* happen, at least much more of the time, greatly reducing problem resolution time?"

As long as you understand that is your very valuable mission, you're off to a good start. Here's what I recommend:

- Assess the extent that problems are *not* solved on their first occurrence.
- Assess the time it takes to solve customer problems.
- Assess the extent of unsolved problems.
- Assess the level of customer dissatisfaction with your current problem-solving processes (they may be accustomed to problem reproduction, etc, and may not be really dissatisfied, but they might be delighted if offered that problem resolution could be performed more quickly).
- Assess the extent of features *not yet* implemented but currently available in your operating system or middle-ware or application (example: UNIX or Windows systems that don't automatically capture storage dumps, but could, with a parameter change).
- Assess the level of duplicated hardware and software for problem repro environments.
- Assess the level of potential customer uptime improvements with first-fault problem solving.

Additionally, you should perform any other assessments that you feel are appropriate to estimate the costs of your current modus operandi, as well as the value to your customers and your own organization by changing its mindset and procedures.

- Provide incentives for reducing the numbers of occurrences, for instances of solving problems on their first occurrence. These do not have to be monetary incentives, but the key point is to encourage the positively changed behavior.
- In your problem management system, specifically track the numbers of times a problem occurs before it is solved.
- Implement platform features for first fault problem resolution that are not yet implemented (for example, more service information directed to customers, or more tracing).
- Publicize the improvements to your processes and products; give the materials to your marketing department, etc. Have white-papers created.
- Change behavior positively, change processes permanently. If a problem requires reproduction, send the incident through Root Cause Analysis (RCA), or other Quality processes to obtain improvements.

In the next chapter we examine the special software and hardware serviceability requirements of our smallest systems, hand-held computers, whose functionality and complexity dwarfs giant mainframes of a few decades ago.

CHAPTER 8 THE SPECIAL NEEDS OF HAND-HELD COMPUTERS, CELL-PHONES, PDAS, AND OTHER SMALL SYSTEMS

"Where a calculator on the ENIAC is equipped with 18,000 vacuum tubes and weighs 30 tons, computers in the future may have only 1,000 vacuum tubes and perhaps weigh 1.5 tons."

Unknown, *Popular Mechanics, March 1949*

Chapter 8 The Special Needs of Hand-Held Computers, Cell-Phones, PDAs, and Other Small Systems

The last fifteen years have seen the rise of very powerful hand-held computers. They have expanded from their origins as offline appointment and telephone number listing devices, to their role as powerful 24X7 online computers with cell-phone, GPS, internet, Wi-Fi, Blue-tooth, and many other network and internet capabilities. With telephone capabilities and users discontinuing land-lines and depending on cell-phones, the cell-phone devices are surely mission-critical for many users – one expects what used to be referred to as always-on *"dial-tone"* telephone-company reliability, as well as state-of-the art innovations.

These small machines are powerful computers, but they are in the hands of consumers, with varying technical skills, little patience or interest in problem-solving and real production needs for systems that work and be restored quickly and easily when problems do occur. The problems that occur in these devices need to be resolved effectively, and, as much as possible, without an external source.

Much of the thinking and methods regarding the nature of software problems, the means of resolving them on their first occurrence, and the kinds of software facilities available to software developers, are still applicable. But several things are different:

- The users cannot tolerate long outages. Quick resolution is necessary. There is no good time for planned outages at headquarters since users expect their systems to be operational 24 x 7.
- The users need a means of resolving problems by themselves as much as possible. Use of the internet is desired.
- The systems are remote from a HQ datacenter.
- The systems have huge install bases (clients)
- The install bases are geographically widely-dispersed
- Except for different user-type applications, the software levels of system and middleware are very controlled (by the vendor), and tend to have comparatively few versions
- Hardware levels are similarly very controlled, although there can be great variety in attached external devices.
- Large or complex data files to solve problems like complete storage dumps or lengthy detailed internal traces, cannot be accommodated at all, for general use.

Hardware and software *self-service*

Since the user set is so diverse, it does include a very large population of technically unskilled personnel, so resolving problems, and especially, first fault problem resolution, often can and necessarily includes workarounds, so the user can keep operating. Performing technical root-cause analysis may be difficult for the end-user, but the headquarters (HQ) team supporting this remote unskilled install base will surely need to be able to detect problems rapidly. The HQ team must do real root-cause analysis and distribute updated software from data made available from this unskilled install base. Diagnostic data must be collected automatically as much as possible.

The install base is all remote, distant from a vendor's main site in a remote data-center: this is a very different environment from the one faced by many software folks who work in an Enterprise data-center, or who develop software for the Enterprise market. The devices must be able to communicate to receive software updates: to support this basic requirement, significant vendor testing is needed for every system software level that is propagated.

The urgent needs of the vendor service organization

Besides the consumer, the user of the hand-held device, the vendor support organization has a very vested interest in finding out how their widely-dispersed customer set is performing, and they need to be notified of problems as soon as possible. They also need to be able to send corrections out as soon as possible. Some systems communicate regularly with HQ and get updated software at regular intervals; some systems, such as cell-phones, need to be updated manually, as initiated by the user, according to very simple instructions. A frequent connection to HQ with status information from the device, with the opportunity to receive software fixes, is very valuable, if performed on a regular basis.

Useful status information for the vendor is: error history (the use of numeric codes - 4, 5, or 6 digits long would be easier for a client, and still have quite a range of sufficient *service points*), average utilization (CPU percent, data storage, networking features), and any significant messages displayed to the user.

Hardware diagnostic information

Many of the problems that can occur in these devices are intermittent, associated with variances in cell-phone, Wi-Fi, and GPS signals – a problem needs to be resolved without powering off the device and powering it back on. Experience has shown that "hangs", where the device is communicating with a network or other device that is hung, or providing a weak signal, is a frequent problem-type.

Hitting *reset*... often...

These kinds of error events can be resolved with a reset of the associated function: if one performed a total power-off followed by power-on that could work too, but the time disruption such an outage would take is really a last resort. Yes, a minute or two is a long time for an individual user, but server outages in an Enterprise data-center may take five or more minutes. Many small cell-phones or hand-held systems have online concurrent resets to use. This reset functionality is found in Apple IPhones, and the Palm Pre, as well as the specially-created US Census 2010 THC hand-held computer, based on Microsoft Pocket PC.

To solve some software problems, a capability allowing a user to restore data or programs to a prior working state is available. The IPhone and THC Census 2010 device allow reloading of data and applications.

Many vendors of these devices provide diagnostic capabilities to verify the correct functioning, and often signal strength of the communication devices. These are surely helpful for users to analyze their own problems and perform their own first-fault problem solving. Palm Pre has two kinds of diagnostic programs – Quick and Detail.

Servicing a *very* large install base

A vendor will have an in-house virtual online scoreboard to keep track of their remote systems, the large user install base, as much as possible, with a history of software levels, errors, changes to hardware and software, etc. Trending of usage issues, including problems, is very valuable, and mining of data is continually needed to be able to proactively support users before they and the system's reputation, get into deeper trouble.

Chapter 8 The Special Needs of Hand-Held Computers, Cell-Phones, PDAs, and Other Small Systems

As is the case for Enterprise-class software, the single best indicator of problems solved, and not yet solved, is the "About" information, containing software and/or hardware version information. A hand-held machine should be able to display this easily to all users.

The hand-held devices have brought new serviceability challenges to software professionals. Many of the features associated with Enterprise-class systems, for serviceability, and first-fault problem solving, are valid and portable ("About", error messages, etc.), but some are not (crash dumps and extensive traces). Large volumes of data for most problem solving, like crash dumps, user dumps, and extensive traces, cannot be used generally (except for a device with a direct connection, such as one to USB).

The crash log

Several vendors have chosen to use a feature commonly called a "crash log". Such vendors include Apple (IPod and IPhone), Blackberry, and Palm (Treo, Pre). This file corresponds to the mini-dump of Microsoft Windows. Essentially, the crash log contains software version information, and active program information; additionally, it should suffice as a level 2 tool – useful for problem screening, and with great information as to the location (failing program) of the current error. The crash log is another form of a problem "signature".

There are new frontiers here for problem representation and signature capture, including uploading it to HQ, all the while keeping much of the details invisible to the users.

In our next chapter, we examine the relief provided by major software vendors in the forms of commercial first-fault software problem-solving products that are already available, and have been used by customers: many have been in production for some considerable time now. All it costs is money, as has been said.

Chapter 8 The Special Needs of Hand-Held Computers, Cell-Phones, PDAs, and Other Small Systems

CHAPTER 9 COMMERCIALLY-AVAILABLE FIRST-FAULT PROBLEM-SOLVING TOOLS

"An apprentice carpenter may want only a hammer and saw, but a master craftsman employs many precision tools. Computer programming likewise requires sophisticated tools to cope with the complexity of real applications, and only practice with these tools will build skill in their use."

Robert L. Kruse, *Data Structures and Program Design*

Purchase it (buy!) or program it (build!)?

Reading this book so far, you have learned the value of first-fault problem solving tools. You are aware of the costs and disadvantages of relying upon problem recreation. From an earlier chapter, you know how to improve software to include first-fault problem solving features.

Also in a previous chapter, managers have been told of a process, to alter the mind-set current for problem-solving at your organization. These modifications could take time and money. Why not *buy* a solution? Could that be cost effective? Could that allow us to be up and running sooner with an improved process? Are there any commercially-available products that would provide first fault problem-solving capabilities?

Yes, there are. There are several categories of products providing this functionality. Is there any *one* product that provides capability to solve *all* problems on their first occurrence? That does not seem possible, unless one runs a virtual machine product tracing *all* guest instructions. This would run very slowly, and still could be very difficult to use effectively. There are some leading-edge future products underway, and they are discussed in subsequent chapters, but for now, there really are many products to choose from, but they are specialized for particular circumstances and environments.

How do you choose? Several thoughts come to mind:

- Consider your organization's *history*, including what kinds of problems you have experienced in the past. Should you, could you obtain a tool to focus on those kinds of problems?
- Consider your organization's *future*. What will be changing in your organization's future: new operating system (or new version/release), new middle-ware, new application or application changes? Your commitment to serviceability will be longer if you invest in a product.
- Consider your experience reports: where do your customers feel the most pain? What problems have the most impact to them?
- Consider *both* improving your organization's own software, and its use of not-yet-implemented first fault features in operating systems, middleware and applications, as well as augmenting what you have with off-the-shelf products. You do not want to fall into the trap of becoming dependent on an external vendor's product while you are underachieving serviceability capability in your own products – you

can fall victim to being highly dependent, forever, on the external vendor.

Purchase it (Buy!)

So, you want to investigate buying a solution to your problem solving needs. It should be noted, before we start, that the companies and products named in this chapter are meant to be representative, only. Major manufacturers are chosen to indicate both the significance of the category, and the company's interest in this kind of production first-fault problem-solving product. But there is no attempt to cover all manufacturers, or to endorse any one company or product over another. But we do have many products, in many categories, to choose from, and actually, many companies are represented here.

The breadth of the products described here does indicate that there are serious, significant vendor solutions to many phases of the first fault problem resolution process – reporting and discovery, data-gathering, diagnosis, ongoing monitoring. The list also shows how software products are offered for a wide breadth of established software platform operating systems: Windows, Unix/Linux, IBM mainframe, and others.

Applicability of a named product to your needs or your organization's needs can only be determined by you and the associated vendor. This chapter and the companies and products named are essentially idea-starters, meant to be thought-provoking. Yes, there is a choice where you don't have to make your own application or operating system to provide the serviceability you choose; you could purchase a product that facilitates this.

There already are tools that provide assists to the several aspects of the problem-solving process:

- Problem discovery (and automatic notification)
- Internal technical data and external data collection
- Data analysis and interpretation and signature creation
- Automated symptom matching

AUTOMATING ERROR NOTIFICATION

Servicelink by Axeda

A tool that can help one create "phone-home" environments for any system is Axeda's Servicelink Applications (Axeda Corporation, 2009). As they describe, it provides an "on-demand remote service connection". It actually is a phone-home application development total environment, with software tools to help you create a complete "phone-home" automation environment, from initial detection of the alarm, to automated reaction to posting in headquarters, to subsequent triggers in headquarters. Axeda affirms that Servicelink will enable your organization to detect and fix problems through proactive monitoring before your customers find their problems.

Their packages include rule-creation (**if** "data-value", **then** "take action") that have supported a wide class of devices in many diverse industries. The package provides complete support including support for the back-end headquarters handling of alerts reported by the monitored devices. Clients include technology, industrial, health-product and other manufacturers.

This package can help with both the speedup of the initial detection and the response to problems (some automated resolutions via rules), as well as headquarters logging of problems. Of course, this can be used for automation assists with software problems, as well as hardware and other kinds of problems, whatever is programmed to be monitored.

Alarmpoint by BMC

AlarmPoint by BMC (AlarmPoint, 2009) is a comprehensive event-notification system that is used to propagate alerts to the engineers and their management. It includes a virtual testing feature to ensure it is primed correctly.

PROBLEM DIAGNOSIS AND ANALYSIS

Problem externals data-gathering

Recording User Screen Contents – "Externals tracing"

Think of this type of tool as the airplane cockpit voice recorder. That cockpit voice recorder helps understand the "big picture" regarding a problem circumstance when analyzing an airplane crash, the "macroscopic" view, but the "data recorder" with various instrument readings gets down to the real internal detailed level, the "microscopic" view. Similarly thinking helps you understand the value of these tools that record a user's screen contents. One could also consider that these tools help match a problem to a prior instance (screening), but sometimes, they can be used to define the externals of a completely new problem, since they trace the "externals" of a problem, versus the "internals" trace provided by internal traces or storage dumps. Still, they can be very helpful to proactively record user interactions reducing the need for, in many cases, eliminating, the need to re-create the problem by the end user.

Microsoft Psr.exe – This feature is expected in Windows 7 (MSDN Windows Developer Center, 2009). It is a tool to trace user screens and responses. If this tool is started at the start of every session, it would be a first fault tool, but if it is invoked only after a problem is first noticed and then recreated, of course we'd call it a second fault tool. In either case, it provides very valuable problem external description information – the screens and responses that precede the problem's occurrence. The accumulated log contains the external conditions that drove the problem.

CITRIX ScreenHistory 1.0 - This feature is available now, and was made available in 2008, as a download from the CITRIX corporation website. It provides capture of the screen image as seen by an individual user. As CITRIX describes it (CITRIX Corporation, 2008), "The ScreenHistory utility helps you troubleshoot issues affecting the GUI, seamless functionality, and so on. This screen capture utility makes troubleshooting and reading other logs/traces easier."

MESSAGE ANALYSIS

Pre-existing operating systems and middle-ware and applications already generate many messages. Recent innovators have thought to better capture and analyze these messages with some valuable knowledge gained about a site. Since messages often communicate what is working on a server, as well as what may not be working, or what might be having intermittent or soft errors, clever use of all of this data communicated to the outside world is very tempting to assemble.

There are many challenges faced by the vendors who develop these products, and many of them relate to no common standards across different platforms or different vendors. But if one is supporting many different vendor platforms at one site, one of these products could be very helpful in getting knowledge out of the glut of message data.

Loglogic by Loglogic

Loglogic (Loglogic, 2009), is a significant recent vendor. The basic concept of continuously collecting pre-existing data for future research and analysis is best shown with this type of product. The product is used to monitor security breaches, data-base access, and compliance management. It supports a large variety of operating system platforms.

LogRhythm by LogRhythm

LogRhythm (Log Rhythm, 2008) is another significant recent vendor that has been welcomed into the technical community (Powell, 2009). It is similar to Loglogic in offering compliance assistance and forensic analysis assistance. In addition to collecting data from pre-existing logs, users can create new events to be monitored.

PERFORMANCE PROBLEM DIAGNOSIS AND ANALYSIS

With performance monitoring products, significant diagnostic data is captured, allowing resolution of many problems, and providing a "second-fault" tool to look for particular conditions to narrow in on the root cause of the software problem. There are many tools that monitor a server's performance (CPU, I/O, network, storage etc) and they also save and permanently record the data they obtain. Analyzing this data, going backwards in time, one can often see the root cause of the performance problem.

Often, a performance problem can develop, and this kind of problem may be even more likely than in the past. Internet connections to a large group of servers mean an incredibly large network of users, and a large rush, in any given time period 24 X 7, making manual monitoring of performance impractical. These tools not only display current performance of many system resources, but allow forensic analysis of archived data, which is valuable when performing root-cause analysis of a problem which occurs intermittently, or develops over time as a gradual capacity utilization increase, or suddenly, due to some complicated unexpected work/resource interactions. Performance monitors can collect and sample data that has already been accumulated internally by the base operating system.

The Microsoft Windows world has seen somewhat very recent strong upgrades and improved offerings regarding performance monitors: Both the Windows "process monitor" and Windows "performance monitor" can now monitor and track hundreds of parameters. They are available as downloads, with contributions from the Winternals company, acquired by Microsoft in 2007.

In the Unix/Linux and z/OS mainframe worlds, those operating systems have integrated performance and usage monitors, with varying data collection. Recent third-party vendors have added data archiving to the Windows world. All platforms have benefited by third party software vendors who have added both backwards and forward analysis. You use the backwards analysis to determine a problem's root-cause and you will use the forward analysis for capacity planning and performance forecasting.

Performance monitors:

- **Compuware Vantage** (Vantage, 2009) - Provides performance management of the end-user environment. The vendor indicates that Vantage's goal is to: "Optimize end-to-end application performance through proactive measurement and reporting".

- **Uptime software's "up.time"** (UptimeSoftware, 2009) – Extensive cross-platform performance monitoring installing their "'agents", minimal monitoring without agents installed.

- **Nimsoft** (Nimsoft, 2009) - Performance and availability monitoring. Nimsoft Monitoring Solutions, formerly called "NimBUS". Includes virtual server support. Described and compared with peers in an Information Week article (Biddick, 2008).

- **Sysload** (Sysload, 2009) – Performance and capacity management solutions. "Ensuring optimum data center service delivery".

- **Resource Measurement Facility** (RMF, 2009) – IBM z/OS includes Work-Delay monitor to analyze why a unit of work is delayed, what resource (CPU, processor storage, I/O, etc.) the unit of work is waiting for. Also has batch and online command support. I/O performance data is obtained from hardware counters in server hardware channels and I/O devices interrogated by the RMF software.

- **IBM Tivoli Performance Analysis** (IBM Corporation, 2009) - Predictive performance analysis.

INTERNET CLIENT/SERVER APPLICATION PROBLEM ANALYSIS

Very highly received, and successful with large install bases, are products that perform first fault software problem solving for internet servers. Notable examples include:

- **BMC Application Problem Resolution** (Application Problem Resolution, 2009) – Application Problem Resolution (formerly known as AppSight) captures, communicates, and pinpoints the root cause of J2EE and Windows .Net application problems down to the code for any specific transaction. This product has a very long production-use history, starting as the Identify product from the Identify company.

- **CITRIX** – EdgeSight (EdgeSight, 2009) – Four products that provide a view of performance from a user's view and from the application, allowing root-cause analysis of performance problems. Support for XEN virtualization and load testing, and **Netscaler** for web application analysis and problem resolution.

- **Computer Associates Wily Introscope** (Introscope, 2009) CA acquired the Wily company. Runs on many following platforms: Windows, IBM mainframe, many UNIX and Linux variants, etc. It monitors all transactions and discovers application dependencies. **CA Wily Customer Experience Manager** is an additional product that allows detailed performance monitoring of individual users.

- **IBM Tivoli Monitoring for Web Infrastructure** (Tivoli Monitoring, 2009) Supported environments include UNIX, Windows, and z/OS mainframe. Provides monitoring of multi-platform web environments.

PROBLEM DATA COLLECTION

HYPERVISORS

Additionally, a product that can trace all instructions within a server, such as a hypervisor, or virtual machine, can be used to record instruction sequences and then back-track to the point where the error starts. As you likely know, a hypervisor is a software product that runs other operating systems as "guest" programs, and the hypervisor virtual machine controlling program (the "host") can trace instructions and activity within the virtual machine. Hypervisors include VMware (acquired by EMC in 2004), Xen, SUN Solaris containers, Hyper-V from Microsoft, Virtual Iron (acquired by Oracle in 2009), and the earliest virtual machine innovation, IBM mainframe z/VM.

AUTOMATED DIAGNOSIS OF ERROR CODES ("ABEND" CODES)

ABENDAID by Compuware

A product whose functionality has expanded over time is Compuware's ABENDAID (ABENDAID, 2009), which provides analysis, at the source code level, and notification of failures for IBM z/OS mainframe production problems. It also allows for real-time as well as archival analysis and reporting of problems. It operates by hooking into the user dump process (abnormal end – "ABEND") and analyzes the dump contents, explaining the meaning of the ABEND code in English, and how the problem corresponds to the user's source code. It helps keep higher-level language programmers from having to analyze hexadecimal storage dumps.

SPECIAL PROBLEM TOOL

Memory Leak tools

IBM Rational for Unix/Linux and for Windows (Rational PuriflyPlus, 2009) – This is a runtime production-level tool to help detect and solve memory leak and other memory consumption production problems.

Summary

There are quite a variety of helpful third-party products which facilitate solving problems as soon as possible. One does have options whether or not to build or to buy their serviceability solutions, but care must be taken to avoid "leaving it all up to the tool", since positive serviceability improvements, discussed earlier, should always be included when building your own products and your own infrastructure. Also, you should never ignore serviceability features that are built into your operating system or middleware, but are unused. In addition, you must be prepared to handle and resolve quickly the problems that were unexpected, that did not occur in the applications, systems, or environments for which you purchased a problem-facilitating solution. What if the unexpected still happens after you bought a 3rd-party tool?

Speaking of the "unexpected", what happens if a problem occurs, and you cannot solve it on that first occurrence? Is that possible? After reading so far into a book called "First Fault Software Problem Solving", that you haven't been able to solve a problem after it occurred once? Yes, it is possible, and until you reach a state of divine perfection, it is likely to happen sometimes. And when it does, you will need to use a "second fault" tool to gather more and more relevant data the next time the problem occurs. To help you in those efforts, you should read the next chapter, devoted to "Second Fault" problem solving tools.

CHAPTER 10 "SECOND FAULT" TOOLS

"In a true zero-defects approach, there are no unimportant items."

Philip Crosby, *Reflections on Quality*

First-fault tools can fail to solve a problem

With everyone's best efforts, following all the previous advice, and continually improving your first-fault problem-solving capability, even the best software serviceability features will on occasion let you down, and you may find that you have a problem that has occurred but you can't solve it. Well, at least, you haven't solved it *yet*!

With the diagnostic data you have collected already, you can use that as a basis for employing a production-level "second fault" tool. A second fault tool is a tool that collects selected diagnostic data according to criteria you create after you have analyzed the first fault diagnostic data. The first fault data gives you a starting point, some starting point: perhaps it is a particular message, perhaps it is a certain error code, or perhaps it is the resource usage, say, CPU usage of a particular application.

The second fault tool will take your starting point, and collect either a single point of data (like an entire storage dump), or multiple points of data up to the error, according to data you already know, as with a tracing tool. The goal is to collect more data describing the problem, and hopefully be able to back-track further in processing to see where the wrong turn, the wrong path in the code, was taken. The big challenge is creating a second fault tool that operates in production (our goal), so work can continue processing normally but if and when the problem reoccurs, you will collect more and better diagnostic data the second time around.

You will either be able to deduce the root cause of your problem or you will surely be able to come closer using the data with the second-fault tool to narrow down the root cause with additional uses of the second-fault tool to catch it on a reoccurrence, soon.

Experiences have shown that one needs to aggressively plan this second engagement to "trap" the problem environment *and* collect diagnostic data sufficient to determine where the fault may lie. It is not unusual for several uses of a second-fault problem resolution tool to be required. It may also be advantageous to try to replicate a problem in a laboratory environment, with non-production laboratory tools operating *concurrent* with setting the production second fault tool.

PROBLEM REOCCURRENCE AND FIRST, SECOND FAULT TOOLS

What one definitely does not want to do is just say, "Well, the problem will reoccur, and *maybe* we will get more or different data on that second occurrence. I sure hope so…" Experience has shown that a proactive approach resolves problems faster. And depending on the laboratory environment alone, abandoning a client to the whims of a production accident, while one tinkers in the lab, is not effective, but it has been done in the past, for sure.

How yucky is system YUK?

We are really including this information about second-fault tools for completeness, because, in fact, second-fault tools are needed. They are used often and one can't always nail that problem's root cause down the first time, every time. However, if we recall the case of System "Yuk", with its terrible diagnostic capability: When System Yuk indicates there is a problem, there really is not much information to go on to create a better data-collection arrangement for that second-fault tool to collect the next time the problem (or any other problem) occurs.

Actually, with System Yuk, your second-fault tool really could be collecting the first set of decent complete information, and with the data you can collect then, you can shape a better set of parameters to trap the *third* instance of the problem occurring, with a better collection of data with the *second* instance of using your Second-Fault tool. Does this make sense? With System Yuk, you surely are always one attempt behind. System Yuk, by itself, is essentially worthless when it comes to getting first fault diagnostic data.

First-fault vs. *second fault* problem solving

If a first fault tool fails to collect significant diagnostic data, how do you know just how bad, how minimal, the data collection was? And how far away from solving the problem are you? Will you ever solve the problem? It is very important to work to maximize the relevance of the data you can capture in your first fault data collecting and collection tools. So, just remember, one should emphasize and encourage first fault problem solving.

So, again, we say, it really pays big dividends to focus strongly on very powerful first-fault capabilities, because without them, our second-fault efforts could start with just so much more of a handicap. Strong first-fault tool data takes us so much farther down the route to problem resolution.

Hacking and *whacking* vs. *scripting*

But yes, second fault tools are needed. In the past, it was automatic to think of "instrumenting the product", which meant creating a customized data collection tool or process. One could force a storage dump by changing the op-code to make an invalid instruction op-code, or branching to the storage location of a bad op-code. Or by creating a program loop with an instruction that branched to itself, you would stop processing in a way recognizable as a loop, and then force a storage dump at that point. All of these methods were very crude, very dangerous to put in place, and always required work to undo. And they were very disruptive to normal processing, besides.

Another method used when you don't have a second-fault production tool, is creating a script or procedure or special program to capture diagnostic data. These specially-developed pieces of program logic tend to be poorly tested, easily forgotten, and they are often recreated in future problems, and if they are saved and re-used, they suffer the risks of other poorly maintained, not updated code – they could cause reliability problems in the name of trying to solve a problem. Thus, specialty "non-supported" throw-away, home-grown serviceability code can be very dangerous. It is far better to devote one's efforts to creating regularly supported and tested second-fault tools, built into your product, the same as the first fault tools that you use. Any temporary custom-built code should be considered for a more permanent status, fully supported, within a tool.

When do I set a second-fault trap?

The question arises: I just had a major problem and some diagnostic data was captured when the problem occurred. I don't immediately have an explanation as to the root cause of the problem. How long should I wait while I examine the diagnostic data before I start planning to implement a "trap" to capture data with the second fault tool? If I wait too long, then the problem could re-occur in production, and I will have missed *that* opportunity to collect diagnostic data. You don't want to do that.

This really requires some true personal multi-tasking, and balancing your use of your time. You want to be able to set up the trap to "catch" the problem with a means of collecting more and better diagnostic data, before you miss that opportunity. If you have a platform which is comparatively rich in Second Fault tools, then it is comparatively easy to set up at least a rudimentary, perhaps not fully refined "trap" to catch additional data if the problem re-occurs.

All along your analysis efforts, concurrently think of what additional data you need and how you may refine or improve or augment your second-fault data capture. Thus, ideally, you will have a second-fault trap active, almost all of the time you are analyzing your current collection of (first-fault) diagnostic data, and you will be regularly thinking of what more data you'd need to solve the problem if it re-occurred. And yes, if your initial collection of data is inadequate (first fault), then you surely will be thinking of trying to recreate the problem faster (in your non-production lab or test system).

Fortunately for many platforms, these days, there are substantial second-fault tools to collect production diagnostic data. And yes, one can keep a second-fault tool turned on continuously, and thus use it as a first-fault tool. This would be easy to do with a tool with minimal performance overhead.

What is minimal performance overhead? This is the biggest question regarding the performance impact of leaving the tool running, but it could be very useful to make a judicious choice of parameters active so as to collect *some* subset of diagnostic data with the second-fault tool. One would guestimate that perhaps a 3 to 5 percent overhead would not be noticed by many users, but site requirements may vary these rules of thumb. This will be especially attractive if, at the time, there is a minimum of automatic first-fault data collection (this is our "to-do", to ensure that we will soon have significant first-fault data collection). This question about performance overhead of second-fault tools mirrors the same discussion and questions regarding the performance overhead of first-fault tools.

EXTERNAL ENVIRONMENT DETAILS AS WELL AS INTERNALS

One may first want to be able to replicate and examine the external environment – the series of screens that a user sees and responds to, before experiencing an error, or other external information. If we recall our classic examples from the airplane industry, "black-box" data recording really refers to TWO collections of diagnostic data: the first is the detailed technical data regarding instrument readings, and the second is the cockpit voice recorder, which has the dialogue and real-time observations of the skilled pilots. This pairing of *internal* and *external* data is valuable, and should be in our minds as we instrument our computers – automation of collection of both the internal and external data would be best.

EXTERNAL CONDITION – SECOND FAULT TOOLS

Tools to capture the external environment include **GoToMyPC** (Citrix Corporation, 2009), that allows remote support personnel to log into a client's PC and see the clients' screens as the users demonstrate the problem occurrence a second time; the support organization can take control for further direct diagnosis. Also, expected with upcoming Microsoft Windows 7 is the **psr.exe** tool (Rose, 2009), which will record a user's screen images and their responses, once started by the client. These are just a brief sample of tools that allow the capture of external conditions when a problem's external parameters are to be captured for second fault analysis.

INTERNAL CONDITION – SECOND FAULT TOOLS

Often the problem is caused by an incorrect path in the code, and one needs to be able to trace, or trace back, how one got there. Thus, there are many internal tools that trace internal software operations.

To trace special events, like system calls, work dispatches, I/O and special detailed technical internal events there is in SUN Solaris, the Unix variant, a very powerful DTRACE (SUN Microsystems, 2009) command to trace many events, non-disruptively, concurrent with production operation. DTRACE is operated via a programming language with which one writes scripts. Sun proudly describes DTRACE as a tool that provides "visibility" into the behavior of the computer software it monitors.

A long-established program is IBM's z/OS Generalized Trace Facility (IBM Corporation, 2007), which captures significant events of I/O, work dispatch, errors, system calls, and "PER" (see below) custom-built recorded events. Some organizations have been known to run GTF trace constantly, as a "first fault" tool, with a subset of available options.

IBM's mainframe z/OS also has a tool to catch particular kinds of error events, SLIP (IBM Corporation, 2007), which captures data and saves it in storage dumps or trace records. The trap specifies error codes (Abnormal termination codes – ABEND codes), the environment in which the error occurs (specific program or application names, user or "kernel" mode, etc), and the associated action to perform (dump, trace, freeze the system), and tailoring options for any data to be gathered. In recent years, SLIP has been improved with functionality to trap the issuance of particular messages, using the message identifier (the z/OS system messages all have message identifiers). There are many more options, but these are the general features.

Some vendors have very specific detail-level tracing operands used when starting a product, or when starting tracing. The level of tracing is sometimes referred to as a "debug level", or often in UNIX, "verbosity". In these cases, the product will collect more and more diagnostic data, the higher the value for the variable. An example of variable amounts of data collection in second-fault tools can be found with CITRIX CDF – Citrix Diagnostic Facility (Citrix Corporation, 2008), which controls debugging options for a number of CITRIX products. Actually, CDF is a front-end graphic means of setting parameters for Microsoft Event Tracing for Windows (ETW) (Park & Buch, 2007). Moreover, ETW allows events and traces generated by user and kernel applications to be recorded.

Help from the hardware

Both Windows and IBM's z/OS (and z/VM) use internal hardware registers to be able to monitor execution of certain programs by address range, branching within those ranges, or storage alteration within an address range. Windows uses the x86 Intel Debug Registers, while IBM mainframes use system ("kernel mode") control registers via the System/z hardware Program Event Recording ("PER") registers. The Windows programs that use the Debug Registers are WinDbg (Microsoft Corporation, 2009) and KD (Microsoft Corporation, 2009); they are applications available in the Microsoft "Debugging Tools for Windows" package. To exploit the PER hardware, IBM z/OS uses an enhancement to the SLIP command mentioned earlier called SLIP/Per, while its mainframe hypervisor z/VM uses a command simply called TRACE.

PERFORMANCE PROBLEMS

A performance problem may be subtle. Often it does not yield a symptom as when something breaks and in turn generates storage dumps or specific error messages. Your CPU, or similar resource, just runs at a higher level than expected. What causes that? One can either perform forensic analysis on previously-collected past data (using a first-fault performance problem-solving tool), or initiate specialized performance tools to focus on particular suspect applications, programs or other defined resources.

For CPU-related performance problems on z/OS mainframes, Compuware's STROBE has been a very highly accepted and utilized tool for some time. It has been popularly called a "hot-spot analyzer". Besides finding programs and resources of high utilization, it provides likely causes with known problems using that program. Example: if it finds high utilization of a floating-point to integer data translation program, it will point out that perhaps an application program has a variable defined incorrectly, requiring frequent data format conversion.

Use of Virtual Machines/hypervisors

Since Virtual Machine technology, like VMware, Xen, Virtual Iron, Microsoft Hyper-V, and IBM z/VM run other (guest) operating systems as application programs, the hosting program, the hypervisor, has incredible power to start/stop/modify its application program (the guest operating system and the applications it runs). Experience has shown how powerful this is in IBM z/VM with a very strong command and tracing capability for recreating and debugging guest problems.

Oh, by the way, you do realize that you should be ready for that major emergency, when you need to use that second-fault tool, right? You should be familiar with the second-fault tools your vendor (and your product) has to offer you, before you set up the parameters on your second fault tool to solve the current urgent "problem du jour".

Firemen go for training long before their first emergency, when they climb up that ladder to reach a fifth-floor fire, save the people on that floor, and put it out. They practice all of those events long before the real thing. If you want to be successful putting out those virtual fires in your data-center or with your product (for you vendors out there), you and your staff similarly must be familiar with your second fault tools. Practice makes perfect.

No matter how successful your first-fault problem-solving endeavors are, you will undoubtedly not solve every major production problem on its first occurrence. You will need to catch the problem as soon as possible on its next occurrence. You should be familiar with the built-in tools in your environment, for second fault data gathering, and be able to operate them to your advantage when you need them.

In our next chapter, we have also anticipated what we hope will become a very rare event, but one for which we must prepare, anyhow, and that is the occurrence that neither first- nor second- fault tools have produced a problem solution. What do we do then? Read the next chapter right now, before your first- and second- fault tools could ever fail you.

By now, you are noticing that this author's solutions have backup solutions, those backup solutions have their own backup solutions. Things happen and you must be prepared. Right? Right!

Chapter 10 "Second Fault" Tools

CHAPTER 11 MAXIMIZING THE VALUE OF DIAGNOSTIC DATA

"We are at the very beginning of time for the human race. It is not unreasonable that we grapple with problems. But there are tens of thousands of years in the future. Our responsibility is to do what we can, learn what we can, improve the solutions, and pass them on."

Richard Feynman (1918 - 1988)

This is a book about solving problems on the first occurrence, and yet the previous chapter is all about what one should do when the first occurrence problem solving is *not* successful. What could be worse than that?

We can add a whole chapter devoted to things you can do when you are really stymied. When does this happen? It happens when the problem makes it through the "gauntlet" – first fault diagnostic data is insufficient to solve the problem, and continued use of second fault tools (previous chapter) fails to narrow down the root cause of the problem.

Really, when can you be in such a state such that you are left completely clueless? When is it likely to happen that you have no idea how to solve the problem? This can happen early in a product's lifetime, when serviceability features are in their infancy. Alternatively, this can happen early in a problem-solver's career. It can also happen when a major change is made in a product and the past serviceability features prove to be inadequate. Theoretically, it can happen anytime, with some major unanticipated problem.

But surely, whenever this happens you will find a way to improve the serviceability (first and/or second fault tools) so you can solve this (and hopefully other similar problems). That is your escape clause, the one that allows you to save face in the light of a real show-stopper-type problem.

In the meantime, long before you have devised a new service tool when your "lesson learned" has not yet been learned, you will need some means of finding a method to think of how you should attack this new problem. You will successfully maximize the value of the data you currently have, for sure.

Many people have been there before you, and many methods have been devised and tested. Realize too that problems that reoccur in production can be solved. Problem reoccurrence, although not pleasant, gives you chances to continually improve your methods and tools. You must take advantage of this opportunity!

This chapter will give a brief survey of some of the more common methods with which you can plan your attack on your difficult problem and resolve it.

Write things down

It is helpful, especially, when starting out as a problem-solver, but continuously, as you work more difficult problems in the future, to write things down. What do you write down? Well, generally, you start by identifying your goal, and perhaps, when you are well-organized, a sub-goal. You should also write down the symptoms you have observed and the results of data analysis you have performed. After that, you also write down the facts you can confirm your hypotheses and the steps you have taken, with results, to confirm those hypotheses. Don't just check things off, but write down your reasons, and your understanding at the time.

You may choose to revisit some steps that are discarded or negated, and good documentation will help you revisit and revise your deductions. And as you work your problem, refer to the things you have written down and add your findings to your document. Modify your plan, when appropriate, as you progress. Additional steps are described in this chapter to help plan solving your difficult problem.

What has changed?

This is the easiest and often the first question to ask.

Pardon me, Isaac Newton, but over time, the thought has occurred that a system that does not change, is at rest and stays at rest, while a system that is not resting in a steady state, goes through changes and experiences a lot of problems. Changes bring problems; an unchanged system that is working does not experience problems, so it seems.

When you work with production software environments, the performance/load and problem behavior of the system may not change much. This is true after the initial production testing is completed and the users have been accessing the system for a comparatively long time. Your system has reached a steady state. Suddenly, you experience some kind of problem.

Perhaps the actual operating environment has changed. It is worth investigating, and to be sure, you must rule out some major change- a software fix, a hardware configuration change, a new application, or new set of users coming online. This is why "change control" (the ITIL/IBM Systems Management process) is so important – it will minimize problems due to changes by ensuring that changes are tested, and have failure data-gathering methods and back-out plans. In any case, good change control will provide you with a log of recent changes to consider in your analysis in the attempt to find the answer to the question: "it used to work. It doesn't now. What *changed*"?

Thinking about "what changed?" may become automatic over time, as a result of multiple experiences, but it is good, when one is starting out solving complex problems, to keep this in mind, early in the problem-solving process.

Troubleshooting techniques: Swap parts, and see if the problem's behavior changes.

A problem solving method often used with hardware parts, which often have an on/off relationship (on = working; off = not working) is swapping parts. You replace a suspected failing hardware part with a new part, and see if the behavior of the whole unit is now working. Also, you could try swapping a pair of like parts to see if the problem changes: an example of this would be with automobiles, swapping the left front tire and the right front tire, and seeing if the steering problem changes. Often this is done with many parts. It is a form of trial and error, but it is quickly done and has very graphic results.

One could apply this to a complex software system. Swap out one software component with another (either at different software "rev" level, or an entirely different compatible component, like swapping out one vendor's version of Linux with another's Linux).

Swapping parts is surely difficult to apply if you have a very complex software system, and no good suspected software parts, or, if the effort to swap software parts via deinstall and reinstall is very time-consuming. Troubleshooting by swapping hardware is surely easier than swapping software.

Given, To Find, Process

Some may remember this method of outlining problem-solving from high school geometry. It was useful then, and it is useful now. Using this method, you will keep track of what you know, what you are trying to find out, and an outline of the method you are using to perform this. It is very basic, but it helps one begin the process of writing things down, when solving a very knotty problem. It forces you to face the data you have, what you need to determine, and to make a written plan for how you will resolve your problem.

5 W's: Who, What, Where, When, Why

Although the 5 W's (Treffinger, Isaksen, & Stead-dorval, 2006) is a technique more often used to recount a story, as a memory-jogger, it can be helpful as you start to solve the current difficult problem. Surely, some of those 5 W's are more meaningful for problem-solving than others (Vostokov, Five golden rules of troubleshooting, 2008). You can also think of them in this form:

- *Who* (or what program) is at fault?
- *What* are the end-results of the defect?
- *Where* in the offending program was the error committed?
- *When* did the error occur? When did the error's effect show up?
- *Why* did the error occur? What is the real root-cause of the error, and what should be done to ensure it doesn't happen again?

In terms of preventing future instances of this class of problem, one should surely solve the *why* of the error's occurrence. One can *resolve* a problem that crashes a server, perhaps, by rebooting that server, but to *solve* the problem, they will need to find the root cause of the problem to prevent the server from crashing again for the same reason.

Polya's techniques

George Polya (Polya, 1957), a famous mathematician, focused much of his time on problem-solving. His contribution involves these four steps:

- **understanding** the problem,
- devising a **plan**,
- **carrying out** the plan, and
- **reviewing/extending** the result.

Perhaps the greatest addition to the techniques described so far is the important point Polya makes to review and extend the results of the problem-solving effort. Our plan is to create FAQs in our database: eventually, perhaps quickly, these will turn into software serviceability improvements. These lasting improvements are how we can use Polya's concept of *extending the result*.

Experiences are also useful regarding the data used/not used to solve the problem, in creating tools and methods for future software problem-solving. Especially, as we seek improvements in first-fault problem-solving, this concept of "extension" is very valuable, as we seek to solve future problems, and prevent future problems. "Extension" provides for continuous improvement.

For example, when you say, "I could have solved the problem sooner if I had XXX data", then you have an extension that could be the basis of a future tool, or the expansion of a current tool.

Additionally, if you say, "We had this software problem in that software component right after the system booted", you invite the extension to your testing efforts to ensure tests are made to additional components right after the system boots. This, you will have new test variations, not only to catch the current problem's reappearance, but other problems with similar characteristics.

Brainstorming

"Brainstorming" is a technique that has been used by many people. Basically, we think of brainstorming as freely listing ideas, often from a group of people. The concept of "brainstorming" was originated actually by Alex Osborn (Osborn, 1948), who founded the early advertising agency BBDO. In his pioneering work, he states that brainstorming referred to "use the brain to storm a creative problem" (Osborn page265). He goes on to say that "judicial thinking must be kept out of such brainstorming". Thus, ideas are to be accumulated, and not edited or judged in the brainstorming session.

Actually, "brainstorming", in its original sense, is far more well defined that just an idea "free-for-all". Four rules keep a brainstorming session on track:

1. **Quantity of ideas** is the initial goal, not their quality.
2. **Criticism or editing of ideas** is not allowed.
3. **Unusual ideas** are to be welcomed.
4. **Combining ideas and refining them** is encouraged.

An individual can do his own modified form of brainstorming, too, but often there is synergy among individuals combining their ideas collectively in a group brainstorming session. The common usage of brainstorming *is* a means of devising ideas in a group. One's statement of a new idea, verbally, can lead to someone else's quick rejoinder, "how about if we also did..."; thus brain-storming is a well-defined but spontaneous group discussion. There are numerous refinements and improvements to the basic brainstorming concept, but no discussion of creative problem solving can omit brainstorming.

Questioning to the void

"Questioning to the void" (Dew, 1998) is a simple, but powerful analysis technique where one continues to ask questions, based on the previous answer. It gets more detailed answers and helps determine the root cause – which is the answer to the last "why" question. You reach the "void" when there is no more "why "question to ask. Here is an example:

The system has crashed.

Question: "**Why** did the system crash?"

Answer: "The system crashed because it was overloaded and running at 100 per cent CPU busy".

Question: "**Why** was the CPU overloaded?"

Answer: "The CPU was overloaded because many more transactions were being received than we usually have."

Question: "**Why** were there many more transactions?"

Answer: "Because our company acquired another company's workers and their workload."

Question: "**Why** didn't we anticipate how much more work would be added?"

Answer: "We didn't know how much more work would be added. We guestimate that we would be all right with the big server that we have."

Question: "**Why** didn't we do a better job of estimating how much CPU resources the additional people would require?"

Answer: "We never had to do that before."

And your conclusion could be: "Maybe we need to have someone focus specifically on *future system performance* or *capacity planning.*"

A similar method of "questioning to the void" is expressed as the Toyota Motors company use of "Five Questions" (Edersheim, 2007). Taiichi Ohno, the originator of the Toyota production system explained, "By asking why five times and answering it each time, we can get to the real cause of the problem, which is often hidden behind more obvious symptoms".

This technique can help you focus on a key anomaly you have found and get all the way to the root cause of that anomaly. You will eventually find the root cause of your problem.

Kepner-Tregoe

Founded in 1958 by Drs. Kepner and Tregoe (Kepner & Tregoe, 1997), the Kepner-Tregoe company today performs instruction and research in decision-making processes. They teach their methods in onsite workshop classes, and have published several books. Their customers include numerous industries, and they have a long list of references of analysis success stories, including problem resolution.

One of their core competencies is a problem-solving process that they refer to as "Problem Analysis". This is likely the best, most widely accepted, with "industrial-strength", highly effective and consistently effective means of solving problems. It can be viewed as a very highly refined process that combines several of the techniques in processes described previously, but with special refinement:

1. Describe the Problem
2. Improve the problem's description
3. Establish possible causes
4. Test the most probable cause
5. Verify the true cause

Answers to the questions, "what, where, when and to what extent" are analyzed according to the following notable characteristics: the detailed answers to the questions regarding what the problem "is" and "what it could be, but isn't", in an attempt to really clarify the exact problem description. The key is the true exact description of the problem.

All Together Now

All together, these various techniques have some common principles to help you work your worst software problem, the one for which insufficient data was captured, and there is no appropriate tool, not yet. This is what we can take away from extracting the most common, and the best features of the above common problem-solving methods:

- There is a large volume of data, some data is more valuable than you currently understand, and possibly some data is not relevant.
- Problem-causing conditions are mixed in with coincidental conditions.
- Writing down what you know, what you need to know and how you plan to get there, and updating your plan with results, is very helpful; it is all but mandatory for a complex problem.
- The data you already have is more significant than you currently realize, although it will take some work to extract its hidden value.
- A combination of creativity in brainstorming possible explanations and deep analysis can be used for best results.
- A very difficult problem's resolution could be accelerated by the efforts of a group, more so than a single individual.
- A solution, and surely, more information, is present for you to find.
- It is necessary to assess your chosen best solution in comparison to the facts of the problem. This is not trivial. Compare your candidate solution to *all* of your observations and conclusions. Any discrepancies should cause you to question if your proposed solution is correct.
- A good problem-solver will make use of his results for future products and processes. The results of the problem analysis that are used far in the future require more than the curt message, "problem closed". There are some very basic guidelines for creating a good report with a value for future improvements, created by an experienced problem-solver (Vostokov, Rules of Analysis Report Excellence, 2008).

The first attempt at formal problem-solving with these methods will be awkward, deliberate, and likely very slow for those first-time users. But the techniques are extremely valuable, and worth investing the time. Managers and mentors should encourage new problem-solvers to learn and use these techniques so good habits can be formed. The new problem-solvers can gain confidence with their success conquering increasingly more difficult problems. Determined problem-solvers are often thought of as individual power-houses, but if a problem solver also has the ability, as a powerful individual, to work synergistically within a group of other powerful individuals on a common problem, and brainstorm effectively with a team, then extraordinary results are possible.

When we accumulate our thoughts in performing these manual problem-solving methods, and we have listed data or tools we would like to have, we have the basis for our future improvements, and the next group of software tools. These future tools will enable us to solve problems more automatically, ideally, on their first occurrence.

Speaking of the future, our next section discusses several aspects of first fault software problem solving in the future. These include leading-edge products, products we'd like to have, trends and opportunity areas for future improvements including unanswered questions and incomplete data, and personally, what we need to do in our own local futures, to better perform first-fault software problem-solving in our own environments.

"The best way to predict the future is to invent it."

Alan Kay

CHAPTER 12 LEADING EDGE SOFTWARE TOOLS

"In the modern world of business, it is useless to be a creative original thinker unless you can also sell what you create. Management cannot be expected to recognize a good idea unless it is presented to them by a good salesman"

David M. Ogilvy

There are a few software tools that are generally available, that have great promise for the future, both in what they do, and the technologies they introduce. There are numerous concepts for future improvements, and they are described in a subsequent chapter.

Instant Replay from Replay Solutions

The first notable tool is called "Instant Replay", from Replay Solutions (Replay Solutions company). It provides a DVR-like (Digital Video Recorder) environment for software problems. It records and makes available, at the internal hardware instruction ("op-code") level, an application. The product was originally created for use by video game-creation, when it was found that it was extremely difficult to recreate a video-game problem by attempting to effectively do-over the hand-motions and reactions to screen images of problem scenarios (Fitzgerald, 2008).

Currently, Replay Solutions has two products, a "Replay Director" and a "Replay Director for J2EE". They point out that they can capture a sequence, and store it in a format such that it can be shared with collaborators, via email, and stored in problem-management systems.

Although there is additional work required to solve the problems whose sequence is captured, additional problem reproduction is not needed. This leads to incredible savings in problem reproduction resources (computers, software, storage, and network) and surely a faster means to solve the problem. Since there is some guesswork and uncertainty involved in any separate problem reproduction process, "Replay Director" is surely more accurate.

ConicIT Mainframe Performance Analysis

ConicIT (ConicIT Corporation) uses artificial intelligence analysis of performance data and messages to anticipate upcoming performance problems. It uniquely learns about performance characteristics of its monitored mainframe systems and thus continuously improves. They say it predicts errors and impending faults. It records its analysis for future further data mining. It also provides for automatic notification of operations staffs for immediate actions.

Continuous learning of software products is a feature that we can expect to see in the future, but this is the only instance found at this point, for first fault problem solving.

Cloud Computing Tools

RIGHTNOW Cloud Computing Monitor

Although this is not a tool that can be used solely to solve website problems when they first occur, it can be very helpful in immediately recognizing the occurrence of a problem. It is a leading-edge tool that uses social networking sites like Twitter, YouTube, and Facebook to mine internet data regarding an organization's websites, their cloud offerings. It is a clever concept based on the recent use of these social networking sites: users have been found to communicate amongst each other regarding a site's problems, in real-time.

RIGHTNOW Cloud Computing Monitor (RightNow, 2009) can not be counted on to be scientific or numerically accurate, but it a very usable additional source of information from a previously untapped source: world-wide users of systems that are "in the cloud". A major benefit: not everyone with a problem reports it to an organization's HELP desk or IT staff, but the RIGHTNOW Cloud Computing Monitor picks up a company's website problems discussed in non-directed, anonymous chatter and buzz. It is a brand-new source of additional data on website problems (Cloud News Desk, 2009).

The Amazon Cloud Dashboard

Amazon also publishes a dashboard with cloud service status (Amazon Web Services LLC, 2009), and status history with brief outage explanations and other data. Details, technologies and tools used by first fault data capture are not visible, but one would expect they exist and are optimized.

CloudWatch from Amazon

Also from Amazon, a new feature, CloudWatch monitoring (Babcock, 2009), is designed to monitor the performance of one's application (EC2) in the Amazon.com cloud.

InternetPulse

To get to a service in the cloud, your request has to travel to the service's website, via the internet (Healey, 2009). And the same is true for your results – they have to travel back from the service's website to your system. The route is imprecise, and perhaps different going and coming for the same transaction. The performance is hard to control and to predict –you do not have a guaranteed route.

There are various means to gauge the performance of the internet. Keynote Systems (Internet Health Report, 2009) has created an online score-board, comparing performance between pairs of internet service provider organizations with data showing current rate of measured transmissions between one Internet Service Provider and another.

Twitter for generalized problem reporting

Twitter represents an interesting use of a global messaging system. Organizations can use the generalized twitter interface for notifying personnel of specific events. Responses can be automated, too. Twitter allows messages of 140 characters or less, but this is not a major limitation. If one combines the value of twitter's reliable message distribution and retrieval system, with the value of a formalized, architected message identifier, then there is considerable value in using twitter for event notification to members of a select global population.

As product first-fault software serviceability gains in importance, we can expect to see more products, more creative products, in the future. These are just a sample of the kinds of thinking possible.

There are areas where some thinking has not been performed, and we have unsolved problems, and solutions whose value has not been numerically computed. As we plan for the future, it is important to understand what we don't completely understand, and that is the subject of the next chapter.

CHAPTER 13 UNANSWERED QUESTIONS

"The important thing is not to stop questioning. Curiosity has its own reason for existing. One cannot help but be in awe when he contemplates the mysteries of eternity, of life, of the marvelous structure of reality. It is enough if one tries merely to comprehend a little of this mystery every day. Never lose a holy curiosity."

Albert Einstein (1879 - 1955)

Questions in general

"Unanswered questions" is our starting point for key questions on the subject of first-fault software problem-solving. This book has described the characteristics of successful systems, how to create and exploit them, and the many advantages and reduced liabilities of solving problems on their first occurrence. Due to the pioneering nature of this work, and the difficulty of performing controlled scientific studies in industry and its user space, there are many questions we'd like to answer, but can't, not yet.

We intuitively think that first-fault problem-solving has advantages, but we may not be able to quantify it formally, and we can't answer many questions. Here are some key questions we know that give us trouble:

- Will we ever be able to solve all problems on their first occurrence?

  (This is surely a dream that, if possible, is very far away, but it has to be mentioned for completeness).

- Is there any operating system/platform with significantly advantageous first fault capabilities? If it is some mainframe operating system just how much more advantageous is it than other operating systems, like a UNIX operating system, or a Microsoft operating system? What UNIX has the best serviceability? Will first-fault software serviceability be expanded in Linux?

We have seen an old Gartner group (IBM Global Services, Product Support Services U.S. (PSS U.S.). , 1998) study from 1998, that points to highest data-center availability from IBM mainframe S/390 (now z/OS), but surely all platforms have changed since then. We infer a connection between first fault software serviceability and system availability, but they are not the same thing.

A very recent survey by ITIC (ITIC Information Technology Intelligence Corporation, 2009), pointed out that IBM AIX running on Power servers had the best reliability, with less than one unplanned outage per year, scoring 99.99% availability (less than 15 minutes downtime per year). The actual statement is (Brodkin): "IBM's Power servers topped a list of most reliable x86 and Unix machines in a new survey, clocking in at only 15 minutes of unplanned downtime per year. Linux distributions running on x86 servers also performed well, as did Sun's Sparc machines and HP's UNIX boxes.

Windows Server machines performed worse than most competitors, with two to three hours of downtime per year, but have still improved dramatically over previous surveys.

Laura DiDio, lead analyst with Information Technology Intelligence, attempted to measure reliability of the most popular enterprise servers. She decided not to include mainframes, which probably would have taken the top spot. "Mainframes are in a class by themselves," DiDio notes. "Whatever you say, you're not taking the mainframe down. It's like the Rock of Gibraltar."

These surveys may be great, but they do not specifically assess the value of one commercial platform's first-fault software problem solving capability. Whatever one may infer from the minimization of downtime, it still does not translate into first fault serviceability. Suppose the systems are very reliable, but serviceability is poor? This does not seem likely at all, but it is possible. A true current (2009) serviceability comparison of all major platforms has not been found, at this point.

- How much messaging should be designed into a new product? What describes too many messages (system TROP), or too few (system YUK)? But practically, how much should one do this, to start with, in their initial designs?
- For developers, when choosing among the available software features like dumps, traces, messages, etc, what is best? What is the best proportion of messages compared to traces or other first-fault features?

- Where will future first fault software problem solving improvements occur (hardware, operating systems, add-on products, and hypervisors)?

- Just how costly is poor serviceability, and little first-fault capability? How much can I save by implementing a process to fully exploit first-fault features at my site or in my products? This question leads us to the really important questions, the ones related to our own connection to first-fault software serviceability.

Questions you can answer at your site

We can answer some of these questions, locally, at our data-center sites, or regarding the software products we have developed. We can do serious mining of our own data, to see:

- How many distinct times do we work on a problem, including reoccurrences in the field, before we have solved a problem? Average number, worst case, and best case?

Perhaps we haven't captured this information, directly. It would surely be worthwhile to prudently change our processes so we can compute these values.

There are additional questions that are necessary to answer:

- Personally, are you convinced that there is great value in deliberately trying to solve problems on their first occurrence, and do you think that there is likely great opportunities to do this at your site, or in your product? If you have any uncertainty, you should consider performing a study. That will be covered in the final chapter.
- Is your organization motivated, or even ready, to change its behavior so problems are solved on the first occurrence? If you are ready, but your organization is not, you will need to come up with personalized data to make the change happen at your site.

We see that although there are many industry-wide unanswered questions, the most important questions, regarding solving software problems the first time they occur, are the personal ones. What is the status of solving software problems at your site, your company, the products you use, and the products you create? You should ascertain the status of the motivation and attainment of first-fault problem solving in your own "sphere of influence", and start a process to continually improve and evaluate it.

As a matter of fact, there are additional ideas and suggestions regarding making improvements in future first fault software problem solving success. They are covered in the very next chapter.

CHAPTER 14 DIRECTIONS AND SUGGESTIONS

"I don't think of laws as rules you have to follow, but more as suggestions."

George Carlin (1937-2008)

Science Fiction

"Science Fiction" could be an alternate title for this chapter. Many readers of the genre have seen that the wild ideas in novels have turned into real events and products. For example, moon exploration ("From the Earth to the Moon" by Jules Verne), and the many inventions of Tom Swift (and Tom Swift Jr.). This is the right time to discuss current trends, and suggestions for future products, to facilitate first fault software problem solving. What is fantasy and impractical today may be implemented in the future. For sure, we should plan for a future filled with improvements.

To review, we have seen that solving problems on their first occurrence is a process that has the following steps, which should be performed as rapidly as possible for best results:

- data collection
- signature creation
- notification
- signature matching to known problems
- deep analysis of data
- complex problem solving
- if there is a failure of first-fault problem resolution, deploy second fault data collection tools
- if there is a failure of second-fault data collection then try again until you must use manual methods to re-analyze your data

       Repeat the above steps...

    ...

- create permanent improvements for FAQs and product features based on this investigation.

In the future, there will be improvements in every step of this process, using more automation, more concurrency, and improved processes and products. We have predictions and high expectations, as well as products, features and services we hope and wish will be created, in the future. They come from seeing how computer software serviceability has progressed, in great detail over the past 40 years; much is done with mere extrapolation from the past into the future. The predictions will be added and described as they relate to the above problem-solving step topic areas:

Data Collection

Fundamental to the start of any software problem investigation is the data to be collected. In the future, more attention will be paid to first-fault problem solving, and generally, there will be more data collected, by all kinds of products, from Enterprise platforms serving a global internet cloud customer set, to individual personal devices. Users will tend to grow in computer sophistication and will be able to reasonably prepare for any required steps for first fault data collection, even if they won't generally be the ones to interpret technical details. The volume of data will grow, as well as the detailed usage, because device capacities will grow. More and more devices, including those personal devices, will be mission-critical, and by necessity, have to be able to capture significant diagnostic data.

There will be more products to automatically capture a product's external interactions with users, to accompany internal problem diagnostic data.

Already, we have seen several recent "screen and mouse motion" capture products from Microsoft and others. This will continue and likely be an automatic and built-in feature.

We can expect more products to better focus on serviceability: architected messages will be created, with message identifiers, expanded use of codes in hand-held devices, and more built-in traces, some created by program development products. Products will create customized storage dump formatters, and much more intelligence will be added to the formatters, such as the "ANALYZE" verb used in Windows and mainframe z/OS crash dump formatters, but a focus will arise trying to solve problems doing everything possible to avoid having to use dump analysis.

A wish for Intel

A wish is that Intel could produce a hardware-support for a software concurrent trace facility, as is done in IBM mainframe z/OS and its related processors. Turning the trace facility ON or OFF could be a user option. Also, optional, would be a setting to trace kernel mode, or user mode operations, or both. Such a facility would be usable by all platforms that depend on the Intel x86 architecture, and thus there would both be facilities that are platform-independent as well as platform-specific features in the trace.

Regarding thoughts on platform-independent features: there are features generally common to all tracing facilities: Maintenance of the table (often a wrap-around table is used) in terms of updating pointers to a next entry. For each entry, you'd want to have a timestamp (almost mandatory), and the value of the hardware's location-counter (the value of the current instruction's numerical address), and also a CPU identification for multiprocessors.

Platform dependent features would include trace entry type, and key registers.

The value of tracing is to be able to back-track to see how you got to a specific point, so key items to trace are the places where control is transferred, either by system calls, I/O operations (sending or receiving), work dispatches and suspensions.

The trace table would appear in a storage dump, and be formatted by platform-specific formatters.

Signature Creation

Initially, this was a manual process, performed with a very basic problem description summary, or signature, created by the problem solver, and manually matched to a private database. Problem signatures were first automatically created by IBM MVS in the early 1980's, and are now found in Microsoft Windows "mini-dumps" (different signatures, of course!). Currently, we have automatic problem signature creation for some products, and we will have better, more comprehensive signature creation in future products, with more automatic signature creation as well. The crash logs of hand-held computer devices are a strong example – and these can be enhanced and improved.

Notification

Much more automated notification of a problem occurrence will be occurring in the future. Right now it is associated with mission-critical Information Technology servers and storage and related devices. In the future, the usage will be expanded to many more devices with embedded computers, both industrial and consumer-oriented. Already, diagnostic medical devices, which are very expensive, can signal when they need service. Features offered by companies like Axeda will make implementation of automated notification more possible.

In addition, users will find they may need to implement their own notification systems as they rely on work offloaded to the cloud. This field will be expanding greatly, as communications through the internet are comparatively inexpensive and downtime is more visible (and easier to minimize) with phone-home systems.

It will be frustrating if a support person is automatically notified of a problem, but has insufficient data to analyze it, or has to contact a user to get it captured. A second choice is to allow the support person to dial in or otherwise connect to the failed system: this is unworkable if the system is down, or has few tools once he connects to proper analyze the data. Thus, automated notification will likely encourage more automated diagnostic data-gathering. One should use the results of the dial-in sessions to go back and improve the automated data collection and analysis. This author has seen this process work successfully.

Signature matching to known problems

Manually created signatures are now replaced with machine-generated signatures. Microsoft is a pioneer in automatically searching its own problem-fix databases upon a user experiencing a major problem, with no user intervention required. In the future, more companies will use this automation feature and Microsoft will likely refine and improve its current process. In addition, they could search other databases besides their own, concurrently, including the internet (all vendors).

The databases to be searched can be expanded. This author has had the concept to use test-case data, extracting problem signatures from a vendor's final test database collection. Then a search of a real customer problem with that expanded database would help isolate the problem to a failing component, and even more, to a failing program. This test-case matching could take place automatically, and it would not have to disclose test-case details to the user. The data-base searching of test data could be viewed only internally by support personnel. It is a means of expanding the set of data to which problem signatures are compared. Why not be able to use test environment problem data/signatures as well as real production problem signatures? This would be especially valuable when a product is newly released and the production problem signature database is sparsely populated.

Also, the database could be expanded with use of the vendor's internal development-organization problem description database, hidden from the end-users. This could also surely help automated early analysis of problems with a new product, where there is little test history.

It is conceivable that one could combine Zeller's automated debugging methods for debugging by test case analysis (Zeller, 2006), with the above concept. This would allow a production problem signature to be matched with failing test-cases, as an additional means of solving production problems (Vostokov, Private correspondence, 2009). This step could be done concurrently, automatically.

Deep Analysis of Data

More vendors will produce storage dump analysis verbs like ANALYZE, used by Microsoft recently, and IBM MVS (z/OS). These verbs do intelligent processing of the data, performing more than just formatting it. They state the relative "health" and anomalies of internal software components, expediting laborious dump analysis work, and actually using the captured expertise of the software experts who know the meaning of various data-values, and their relationships, for each component so analyzed.

Expect Artificial Intelligence and Expert systems to produce better analyses of data. There is room for a lot of improvement and innovations in this category.

Complex Problem Solving

In the case of needing to perform a manual method of solving a difficult software problem (see Chapter 11 Maximizing the Value of Diagnostic Data), for which you have very insufficient first-fault data, and have poor luck with second-fault tools, you will have to perform one of those analytic methods. This author has used basic computer tools to help use Kepner-Tregoe-type methodology, and there are opportunities for more tools like that, that can easily mesh with a problem-management system, as well as software diagnostic data. There is a lot of work to be done, to develop a standardized methodology, and to create one at your organization and get it accepted and integrated into your work flow.

OUT-OF-THE-ORDINARY METHODS FOR PROBLEM-SOLVING

In addition, there will be more creative uses of diagnostic data, and more problem- solving of more complex problems. There are other characteristics of problem-solving we can improve. They include:

- **More concurrency in the problem-solving process** above. We can look to a very easy concept to understand. The General Motors company OnStar (PRNewswire, 2009) organization provides analysis of initial car crash data to be able to convey likely injuries to medical emergency support (paramedics, among others). They accomplished this with a partnership with the USA Center for Disease Control (CDC). Without this feature, a crash gets instantly reported, but emergency medical analysis would start later, at the moment that the paramedics physically arrive at the site; now proper medical service planning and actions can start moments after the crash (Easley, 2009).

- **Non-failure use of trace data**. Recalling back to the start of industrial black-boxes, the airplane industry, there was a recent article describing the air travel industry's use of the data collected for "black-boxes" to improve flight paths for landing, thus preventing problems (Wald M. , 2007). If more and more computer state data is to be collected, and it can be used for non-error situations, besides generally making the data more useful, it will help justify and extend the value of data collection in general, if "emergency data collection" is also used pro-actively, in many "non-emergency" situations.

- **Use of the residual data produced after a major problem, including using the nature of the data and the time it is produced, to creatively back-track the exact kind of fault created**. Perhaps this is a wild idea, but it tries to cleverly use data produced not right at the time of the error, but data that may continue to be generated long after the error occurs. This could be of use for systems that need to stay up, if the error did not totally stop processing. This concept is following the example of the ASA software company's (Air France Flight 447 Recovery Assisted by U.S. Coast Guard and Advanced Search & Rescue Technology , 2009) being able to back-track to the location of an event in the ocean that leaves debris, by using previous weather and ocean current information for each item retrieved at various points in time.

Recently, their simulation program was used to help the efforts to find the location of the downed Air France jetliner on June 1 2009, off the coast of Brazil, using the location and time of discovery of materials that have risen from the airplane.

There will be many improvements in the products used to solve software problems on their first occurrence. This is a very wide open area for research and industry where progress is matched by the complexity and scope of new problems.

Thus, we have discussed what we expect to see in the future. The future is filled with opportunities and more technologies and products in our attempt to come closer to solving every problem as soon as it occurs. We are nearing the end of our journey, from primitive problem-solving to near-perfection in the future. Now, just where have we been on this whirlwind ride through critical software problem solving? It is time to summarize, and read-back the trace of our path through advanced problem solving. On to our last chapter, where we will draw all of our lessons learned together.

CHAPTER 15 SUMMARY

"It is not really difficult to construct a series of inferences, each dependent upon its predecessor and each simple in itself. If, after doing so, one simply knocks out all the central inferences and presents one's audience with the starting-point and the conclusion, one may produce a startling, though perhaps a meretricious, effect."

Sir Arthur Conan Doyle (1859 - 1930), Sherlock Holmes in
The Dancing Men

Taking stock of where we are now

At this point, we have proven that many technologies exist, and more are being created to solve software problems the first time they occur. We have described arguments with which you can convince your colleagues (employees, management, co-workers) to ensure that first-fault problem solving is a part of your business operations, and the products and processes you use and create.

You know that even if you are outsourcing work to other organizations, either away in the cloud or locally, you still are left with a responsibility to be aware of problems and to ensure problems are resolved as soon as possible. Regarding first-fault serviceability, you surely know how to collaborate with the outsourcers, and even advise them, so your problem resolution is handled to your best advantage.

You are more aware of tools that can be used, and several vendors that produce them. You are aware of commercially-available products and the vendors who market them. When tools fail, you are more aware of additional problem-solving methodologies that can be used by you and your colleagues to redirect the unsolvable problem back on track to resolution.

Is the airplane black-box due for changes?

So, the airplane industry is our guiding light, our example, leading us into the future, with extensive tracing, many years before this was implemented to any degree in computer systems? This is true, but in some sense, we in the computer industry have progressed, in some aspects of first fault problem solving such that we can now lead the airplane industry to some improvements.

Specifically, as a result of the Air France flight 447 June 1 2009 crash, where the black box was not located before the automatic radio "ping" was due to expire, there has been a chorus of suggestions for changing airplane black-boxes (Negroni, 2009). Suggestions have included being able to jettison a separately-attached black-box as done successfully in some military aircraft, and also to regularly "phone-home" the detailed data from the black box. Technology progresses and one group can surely learn from another's examples. The airplane industry can learn from the computer industry, but can your organization learn and improve their capabilities for first fault problem solving?

Taking Action in your Organization

I hope that you now know more about this topic than you did before. Your last step is to put this into action, and actually make "first-fault software problem solving" a specific core competency and focus of your organization's problem solving process.

To this end, an evaluation should be performed. For sure, you likely have some anecdotal evidence, some recent past problem "showstopper", that had a great impact on your organization; you have a clue that problem resolution is not perfect. You should perform a more comprehensive, real first study of your attainment in software first fault serviceability.

You need an outside point of view, "fresh eyes," so to speak. An outside facilitator (external to your organization is best) could come into your organization, and lead an analysis study. You could hire an outside expert to analyze your site or product for first-fault software serviceability, also. After you have performed this first evaluation, your own in-house quality-focused people could perform additional regular evaluations: the first evaluation, your "kick-off" into this process, should use an outside facilitator. If you have a large organization and application-set, you may choose to evaluate a particular critical sub-set of the work, for a prototype study.

Some things you would want to evaluate are:

- Do we specifically count the numbers of attempts it takes to solve a problem? If not, our study will be more difficult. This is an area for improvement in our problem management system.
- How often do we solve problems on our first attempt?
- How many problems depend on further analysis – problem reproduction, waiting for reoccurrences, recreation by outside vendors, etc? It would be great to accumulate these different problem recreation events by what type they are: waiting for a reoccurrence, specific problem recreation done by your organization, problem recreation in a vendor laboratory, etc.
- What is the cost of problems not solved on the first occurrence? Computer person-hours, calendar elapsed time, business impact (downtime due to additional outages, users unable to perform their work and their lost productivity, financial impact, etc.)
- What facilities for first-fault software problem solving do you have that are unused? You may need further research with your software

vendors. What benefit could be applied to the sample of problems examined, if your organization activated the features that are not yet implemented?

- Could you use additional commercial products? What benefits would they provide?
- What would be the cost versus the value of improving first-fault serviceability of your own in-house-developed software (applications or systems software)?
- What benefits could you expect to see by:
  - Improving your current processes?
  - Activating unused features?
  - Obtaining commercial first-fault software serviceability products?
  - Updating your own software with selective first-fault software serviceability features?

Surely, your organization has a bright future ahead, being able to resolve software problems as soon as possible, on their first occurrence, now much more quickly than before you read this book. More first-fault software facilities are on the way, but so are many more systems, some more complex than we have now, and others that are much more widely distributed to ever more-demanding users. Improvement must be continuous, and until the day when the last problem is solved, you'll find frequent opportunities to apply the tools and techniques you've learned in this book to your software products and services.

BIBLIOGRAPHY

(2008,). Retrieved September 15, 2009, from Log Rhythm: http://logrhythm.com/

ABENDAID. (2009, July 6). Retrieved July 6, 2009, from Compuware: http://www.compuware.com/solutions/abend-aid.asp

Agans, D. J. *Debugging: the nine indispensable rules for finding even the most elusive software and hardware problems.* AMACOM Division American Management Association.

Air France Flight 447 Recovery Assisted by U.S. Coast Guard and Advanced Search & Rescue Technology. (2009, June 9). Retrieved July 1, 2009, from http://www.asascience.com/news/releases/2009/pr09-AirFrance447Search.shtml

AlarmPoint. (2009, July 6). Retrieved July 6, 2009, from AlarmPoint by BMC: http://www.bmc.com/products/product-listing/6923337-9668-1804.html

Altman, A. (2009, January 16). *Chesley B. Sullenberger III.* Retrieved July 6, 2009, from time.com: http://www.time.com/time/nation/article/0,8599,1872247,00.html

Amazon Web Services LLC. (2009, July 5). *Service Health Dashboard.* Retrieved July 5, 2009, from Amazon Web Services: http://status.aws.amazon.com/

Application Problem Resolution. (2009, July 6). Retrieved July 6, 2009, from BMC: http://www.identify.com/products/index.php

Associated Press (AP). (2009, April 14). *Mars rover has unexplained computer reboots.* Retrieved from MSNBC: http://www.msnbc.msn.com/id/30207796/

Auslander, M. A., Larkin, D. C., & Scherr, A. L. (1981). The Evolution of the MVS Operating System. *IBM Journal of Research and Development*, 471-482.

Axeda Corporation. (2009, July 6). *Axeda Servicelink Applications.* Retrieved July 6, 2009, from Axeda Corporation: http://www.axeda.com/products_applications.htm

Babcock, C. (2009, May 18). *Amazon Adds CloudWatch Monitoring, Other Services.* Retrieved July 1, 2009, from Information Week Business Technology Network: http://www.informationweek.com/cloud-computing/article/showArticle.jhtml?articleID=217500680&cid=nl_IWK_cloud_html

Biddick, M. (2008, February 13). Application Performance Management - APM "Rolling Review Wrap-Up: APM Suites'. *Information Week online .*

Brodkin, J. (n.d.). *IBM Power servers most reliable in new survey They clocked only 15 minutes of unplanned downtime per year.* Retrieved from Computerworld Servers and Data Center: 2009

Brue, G., & Launsby, R. G. (2003). *Design for Six Sigma.* McGraw-Hill Professional.

Citrix Corporation. (2008, October 14). *article CTX104578 - Using Citrix Diagnostic Facility and the Access Suite Console for Tracing.* Retrieved July 7, 2009, from Citrix Knowledge Center: http://support.citrix.com/article/CTX104578

Citrix Corporation. (2009, July 7). *Product Overview.* Retrieved July 7, 2009, from GoToMyPc: https://www.gotomypc.com/en_US/forYou.tmpl

CITRIX Corporation. (2008, November 5). *ScreenHistory 1.0 for 32-bit and 64-bit platforms .* Retrieved July 23, 2009, from CITRIX Knolwedge Center: http://support.citrix.com/article/ctx113046

Cloud News Desk. (2009, May 27). *RightNow Unveils New Cloud Monitor and Enterprise Analytics with RightNow May '09.* Retrieved from Cloud Computing Conference and Expo: http://cloudcomputingexpo.com/node/977954

Compuware Corporation. (n.d.). Retrieved July 6, 2009, from Strobe Extended Play: http://www.compuware.com/solutions/strobe.asp

ConicIT Corporation. (n.d.). *Overview.* Retrieved July 7, 2009, from ConicIT Corporation: http://www.conicit.biz/e/index.php?option=com_content&task=view&id=15&Itemid=34

Covey, S. R. (1989). *The 7 Habits of Highly Effective People.* Free Press.

Croy, M., & with Laux, D. (2008). *Are We Willing To Take That Risk? 10 Quesitons Every Executive Should Ask About Business Continuity"*. IUniverse.

Dew, J. R. (1998). *Managing in a Team Environment*. Quorum Books.

Easley, S. (2009, May 20). *News release: Health Experts Link Automotive Technology To Life-Saving Crash Response* . Retrieved July 1, 2009, from CDC Foundation: http://www.cdcfoundation.org/pr/2009/HealthExpertsLinkAutomotiveTechnol ogy.aspx

Ebbers, M., Comte, P., Corona, A., Guilianelli, J., Lin, D., Meiner, W., et al. (2008). *System z Strengths and Values*. IBM Corporation.

Edersheim, E. H. (2007). *The Definitive Drucker*. New York, NY: McGraw-Hill.

EdgeSight. (2009, July 6). Retrieved July 6, 2009, from CITRIX Corporation: http://www.citrix.com/english/ps2/products/product.asp?contentID=25119

Fagan, M. (1976). Design and code inspections to reduce errors in program development. *IBM Systems Journal , 15* (3), 182-211.

Fitzgerald, M. (2008, March 23). How Did Your Computer Crash? Check the Instant Replay. *New York Times* .

Fogiel, M. (1991). *The Computer Science Problem Solver: A Complete Solution Guide to Any Textbook*. University of Michigan.

Freedman, D. P., & Weinberg, G. M. (1990). *Handbook of Walkthroughs, Inspections, and Technical Reviews for Programs, Projects, and Products*. Dorset House.

General Motors. (2009). *Event Data Recorders*. Retrieved July 2, 2009, from General Motors Safety Initiatives: http://www.gm.com/corporate/responsibility/safety/event_data_recorders/

Goodliffe, P. (2007). *Code Craft: The Practice of Writing Excellent Code*. No Starch Press.

Harler, C. (2007, June 29). *The Trouble With Troubleshooting With So Much Time Spent Finding Problems, Troubleshooting Is A Burden Itself.* Retrieved July 2, 2009, from Processor Magazine - online version: http://www.processor.com/editorial/article.asp?article=articles%2Fp2926%2F 32p26%2F32p26.asp

Healey, M. (2009, March 23). Cloud Computing and Serviceability: "Beat The Slow Commotion: Sluggish Performance is a major headache for user of cloud-based apps". *Information Week* , pp. 40-42.

IBM Corporation. (2007). GTF - Generalized Trace Facility. In *z/OS V1R9.0 MVS Diagnosis Tools and Service Aids.*

IBM Corporation. (2009, August 26). *IBM Tivoli Performance Analyzer.* Retrieved August 26, 2009, from IBM Software Tivoli Products: http://www-01.ibm.com/software/tivoli/products/performance-analyzer/

IBM Corporation. (1994). MVS/ESA SP V4 Assembler Programming Guide.

IBM Corporation. (2007). Setting a SLIP Trap. In *z/OS V1R9.0 MVS System Commands.*

IBM Corporation. *So You Want to Estimate the Value of Availability?*

IBM Corporation. (2008). *z/OS V1R10.0 MVS DIagnosis: Tools and Service Aids.* IBM Corporation.

IBM Global Services, Product Support Services U.S. (PSS U.S.). . (1998, October 29). *"Platform Availabilility Data: Can You Spare a Miinute?".* Retrieved June 29, 2009, from http://www.gartner.com/webletter/ibmglobal/edition2/article4/article4.html: http://www.gartner.com/webletter/ibmglobal/edition2/article4/article4.html

IBM Global Services, Product Support Services U.S. (PSS U.S.). (1998, Oct 29). Retrieved June 29, 2009, from http://www.gartner.com/webletter/ibmglobal/edition2/article5/article5.html

Information Technology Intelligence Corporation. (2009, April 29). *Application Availability, Reliability and Downtime: Ignorance is NOT Bliss.* Retrieved July 16, 2009, from ITIC - Information Technology Intelligence

Corporation: http://itic-corp.com/blog/2009/04/application-availability-reliability-and-downtime-ignorance-is-not-bliss/

Internet Health Report. (2009). Retrieved July 7, 2009, from Keynote Systems: http://www.internetpulse.com/

Introscope. (2009, July 6). Retrieved July 6, 2009, from Computer Associates: http://www.ca.com/us/application-management.aspx

ITIC Information Technology Intelligence Corporation. (2009, July 7). *ITIC 2009 Global Server Hardware & Server OS Reliability Survey Results.* Retrieved July 17, 2009, from ITIC Information Technology Intelligence Corporation: http://itic-corp.com/blog/2009/07/itic-2009-global-server-hardware-server-os-reliability-survey-results/

Kepner, C. H., & Tregoe, B. B. (1997). *The New Rational Manager.* Kepner-Tregoe.

Korach, M., & Mordock, J. (2008). *Common Phrases, 2nd: And Where They Come From.* Globe Pequot.

L3 Aviation Recorders. (2009, July 2). *History of Flight Recorders.* Retrieved July 2, 2009, from L3 Corporate Website: http://www.l-3ar.com/html/history.html

Loglogic. (2009). Retrieved July 6, 2009, from Log Logic corporate website: http://www.loglogic.com/

Loveland, S., Miller, G., Shannon, M., & Prewitt, R. (2004). *Software testing techniques: finding the defects that matter.* Cengage Learning.

Marquis, H. (2009, July 5). *ITIL Service Outage Analysis (SOA) in 7 Steps.* Retrieved July 5, 2009, from ITIL News: http://www.itilnews.com/index.php?pagename=ITIL_Service_Outage_Analysis_SOA_in_7_Steps

Microsoft Corporation. (2009). *Debugging Tools for Windows KD.* Retrieved July 7, 2009, from Microsoft Developer Network: http://msdn.microsoft.com/en-us/library/cc266319.aspx

Microsoft Corporation. (2009). *Debugging Tools for Windows WinDbg.* Retrieved July 7, 2009, from Microsoft Developer Network: http://msdn.microsoft.com/en-us/library/cc266321.aspx

Microsoft Corporation. (2009). *How WER Collects and Classifies Error Reports*. Retrieved July 1, 2009, from Windows Hardware Developer Central: http://www.microsoft.com/whdc/winlogo/maintain/WER/ErrClass.mspx

Mosteller, W. S. (1981). *Systems Programmer's Problem Solver*. University of Michigan.

MSDN Windows Developer Center. (2009, May 20). Retrieved July 6, 2009, from Microsoft.com: http://msdn.microsoft.com/en-us/library/dd371782(VS.85).aspx

Myers, G. J. (2006). *The Art of Software Testing*. Wiley-India.

Negroni, C. (2009, July 14). Building a Better Black Box. *New York Times* , p. B6.

Nimsoft. (2009, July 6). Retrieved July 6, 2009, from Nimsoft Performance and Availability Solutions: http://www.nimsoft.com/index.3.php

Osborn, A. (1948). *Your Creative Power: How to Use Imagination*. London, United Kingdom: Charles Scribner's & Sons.

Park, D. I., & Buch, R. (2007, April). *Event Tracing Improve Debugging And Performance Tuning With ETW*. Retrieved July 7, 2009, from Microsoft Developer Network Magazine: http://msdn.microsoft.com/en-us/magazine/cc163437.aspx

Polya, G. (1957). *How to Solve It*. Princeton University Press.

Powell, J. (2009, September 15). *Q&A: Breaking the Log Barrier: Logs must do more than just record the facts*. (J. E. Powell, Ed.) Retrieved from Enterprise Stragegies: http://esj.com/articles/2009/09/15/breaking-log-barrier.aspx

PRNewswire. (2009, May 20). OnStar Creates Injury Severity Prediction to Improve Automatic Crash Response. *New York Times* .

Rational PuriflyPlus. (2009, July 6). Retrieved July 6, 2009, from IBM: http://www-01.ibm.com/software/awdtools/purifyplus/

Replay Solutions company. (n.d.). Retrieved June 29, 2009, from http://wwww.replaysolutions.com/technology: http://wwww.replaysolutions.com

RightNow. (2009, May). *RightNow CRM Suite: Cloud Monitor*. Retrieved July 1, 2009, from RightNow - On Demand CRM Software: http://www.rightnow.com/crm-suite-cloud-monitor.php

RMF. (2009, July 6). Retrieved July 6, 2009, from IBM: http://www-03.ibm.com/servers/eserver/zseries/zos/rmf/

Rose, S. (2009, July 7). *Tip: Easier Troubleshooting Support with Problem Step Recorder*. Retrieved July 7, 2009, from Microsoft TechNet: http://technet.microsoft.com/en-us/magazine/dd464813.aspx

Scott, D. (1999). *Making Smart Investments to Reduce Unplanned Downtime*. RAS Services. Gartner Group .

Siewiorek, D. P., & Swarz, R. S. (1998). *Reliable Computer Systems: Design and Evaluation*. A K Peters, Ltd.

Skwire, D. (2007, December 4). *Best Practices for Solving Problems in Non-z/OS Environments: How problem solving is different in mainframe and non-z/OS environments, and how you can accelerate troubleshooting convergence.* . Retrieved June 29, 2009, from Enterprise Strategies Journal: http://esj.com/articles/2007/12/04/best-practices-for-solving-problems-in-nonzos-environments.aspx

Sperling, N. (. (2009, July 14). Home Page. *The Journal of Irreproducible Results* . (N. Sperling, Ed.) San Mateo , California , USA.

Stolper, S. A. (2007, August 8). *The software detective: first-fault data capture*. Retrieved July 2, 2009, from embedded.com: http://www.embedded.com/design/testissue/201201766?_requestid=458876

SUN Microsystems. (2009, July 7). *Solaris Dynamic Tracing - Increasing Performance Through Complete Software Observability*. Retrieved July 7, 2009, from SUN Microsystems Solaris Operating System: http://www.sun.com/software/solaris/ds/dtrace.jsp

SUN Microsystems. (2009, July 5). *SUN Services Tools Bundle*. Retrieved July 5, 2009, from SUN Microsystems: http://www.sun.com/service/stb/

Sysload. (2009, July 6). Retrieved July 6, 2009, from Sysload: http://www.sysload.com/

Tivoli Monitoring. (2009, July 6). Retrieved July 6, 2009, from IBM: http://www-01.ibm.com/software/tivoli/products/monitor-web/

Treffinger, D. J., Isaksen, S. G., & Stead-dorval, B. K. (2006). *Creative Problem Solving: An Introduction*. Prufrock Press.

UptimeSoftware. (2009, July 6). Retrieved July 6, 2009, from http://www.uptimesoftware.com/

Van der Linden, P. (1994). *Expert C Programming: Deep C Secrets*. Prentice Hall PTR.

Vantage. (2009, July 6). Retrieved July 6, 2009, from Compuware: http://www.compuware.com/solutions/vantage.asp

Vostokov, D. (2008, Oct 28). *Five golden rules of troubleshooting*. Retrieved July 23, 2009, from Crash Dump Analysis: http://www.dumpanalysis.org/blog/index.php/2007/11/26/five-golden%20rules-of-troubleshooting/

Vostokov, D. (2009, July 21). Private correspondence. Dublin, Ireland.

Vostokov, D. (2009, July 21). Private correspondence with Dan Skwire regarding testing serviceability. *email* . Dublin, Ireland.

Vostokov, D. (2008, October 28). *Rules of Analysis Report Excellence*. Retrieved July 23, 2009, from Crash Dump Analysis: http://www.dumpanalysis.org/blog/index.php/2008/10/28/im-rare/

Wald, M. (2007, October 1). Fatal Airplane Crashes Drop 65% . *New York Times* .

Wald, M. L. (2009, January 15). *New York Times*. Retrieved July 5, 2009, from nytimes.com: Plane Crew Is Credited for Nimble Reaction

Wilding, M., & Behman, D. (2006). *Self-Service Linux - Mastering the Art of Problem Determination*. Prentice Hall - Professional Technical Reference.

Zeller, A. (2006). *Why Programs Fail: A Guide to Systematic Debugging*. Morgan Kaufmann.

THIS PAGE INTENTIONALLY LEFT BLANK

www.ingramcontent.com/pod-product-compliance
Lightning Source LLC
LaVergne TN
LVHW022317060326
832902LV00020B/3524